INTRODUCTION

This book is about a period of history when Britain was the largest superpower in the world. It had the greatest empire, covering one fifth of the globe and contained a quarter of the world's population. It was protected by the largest navy, produced more iron and steel than any other country and led the world technologically with its steam engines.

Britain was ruled by Queen Victoria, a remarkable woman who reigned for 64 years, during which time Britain prospered and the lives of ordinary men and women changed dramatically. Huge industrial towns and cities emerged connected by a vast network of railways, roads and canals. There were significant advances in technology, medicine, education, social welfare, politics and worker's rights.

When Victoria died in 1901 she was much loved and admired. She will always be remembered as one of the greatest British monarchs and as the woman who gave her name to her subjects, the Victorians.

CONTENTS

	Page
Queen Victoria	3
The British Empire	5
The Empire at War	7
A Wealthy Nation	9
Family Life	11
The Poor	13
Education and Social Reform	15
Art and Entertainment	17
Our Victorian Inheritance	19
Giant Victorian Word Search	21
Timeline and Glossary	22

Written & illustrated by William Webb
Front cover illustration by Les Ives
Published by Colour History Ltd © 2006
Print reference number 28464/10/07

QUEEN VICTORIA

Victoria probably never expected to become the Queen of England, as she was fifth in line to the throne. She succeeded her uncle, William IV, who died in 1837 leaving no legitimate heir.

Queen Victoria Marries her German Cousin

The young Alexandrina Victoria spoke with a German accent because her mother was of German origin. She enjoyed music, dancing, sketching, riding and she spoke German and French fluently. She kept a diary from the age of 13 years old until she died. However, she had a strict upbringing and only a few friends. At the age of 18 she became Queen and was crowned the following year at Westminster Abbey in 1838. The Liberal, or 'Whig' Prime Minister Lord Melbourne, advised her to marry quickly to produce heirs to the throne. So, just two years later she married her first cousin Prince Albert of Saxe-Coburg-Gotha. The wedding took place at St James's Palace, the reception at Buckingham Palace and their honeymoon was at Windsor Castle for three days. They were both just 20 years of age.

The Grandmother of Europe

Prince Albert was tall, intelligent and a trusted advisor to Queen Victoria. Like the Queen he cared about the plight of the poorer classes. The couple had nine children and enjoyed family life. Until Albert's death from typhoid in 1861 they were constant companions. Her children, 40 grandchildren and 37 great-grandchildren were married to various European royals. By the end of the 19th century Victoria was related to the royal families of Germany, Norway, Sweden, Greece, Spain, Romania and Russia! She was known affectionately as 'the grandmother of Europe'.

Queen Victoria and Government

Queen Victoria took a keen interest in the government of the country, even though she was a 'constitutional monarch', which meant that Parliament had the bigger say in how the country was governed. She got on well with most of the leading politicians of the day, particularly the Conservative Benjamin Disraeli, who wanted to expand the Empire. She disliked Liberal Prime Minister William Gladstone, who held his post four times during her reign. He was more interested in introducing social reforms to Britain.

The Melancholy Queen

When Albert died, Victoria retired from public life and went into mourning for 13 years and wore black until her own death. Every night Albert's clothes were laid out on his bed at Windsor, each morning fresh water was placed in his basin.

The Queen refused to open Parliament each year and was nicknamed 'the Widow of Windsor'. It was Disraeli who finally persuaded her to return to public life. At the time of her Diamond Jubilee in 1897 Victoria was at the height of her popularity, but she was very frail with poor eyesight, bad rheumatism and was confined to a wheelchair. Even so, the Queen continued to perform her duties until a few weeks before her death. She died at Osborne House and was buried next to Albert in his mausoleum at Frogmore in Windsor.

Prince Albert

> **Prince Albert designed some of the royal palaces. Design your own palace and decide whether you want to use it for private holidays, or for entertaining important guests. You can include gardens or grounds if you like. Draw it in plan form showing the rooms, or as an 'artist's impression' or view from outside.**

The Royal Palaces

Victoria and Albert liked to use some royal palaces for official duties and some as private retreats. They favoured Buckingham Palace in London for government functions, although Victoria thought it was a cold house. In 1844 the couple bought an estate on the Isle of Wight and Albert designed and built Osborne House there. They used this home to get away from their busy life in London. In 1853 Albert purchased and re-designed Balmoral Castle, Victoria's favourite home, in Aberdeenshire in the Scottish Highlands. It is surrounded by mountains and set in 30,000 acres of deer forest. Windsor Castle was built by William the Conqueror in 1066 and is the oldest inhabited castle in the world. It is also the oldest royal palace and during Victoria's reign it was greatly transformed.

Balmoral Castle

Windsor Castle

Osborne House

Buckingham Palace

THE BRITISH EMPIRE

At the start of Queen Victoria's reign, Britain already governed large areas of countries such as India, Canada, Australia and New Zealand. By the end of her reign and driven by the need to find new trade markets, the British Empire became the largest the world had ever seen.

The 'Jewel in the Crown'
Britain imported raw materials such as cotton, tea, sugar and rubber and exported manufactured goods like cotton cloth, locomotives and machine tools to the colonies. For the Victorians it was India which symbolised the Empire. The Queen called it 'the jewel in the crown'. It had an Anglo-Indian army, a large civil service and native officials in government. In 1857 the Indian troops, or 'sepoys', mutinied and shot their British officers, but the rebellion was ruthlessly crushed. From that time India was governed directly by the British government and in 1876 Victoria was proclaimed 'Empress of India'.

A Worldwide Network of Ports
Britain needed to control certain areas which were important trade routes. She acquired Gibraltar, the Suez Canal in Egypt, which created a shorter route to India, Aden, the islands of Hong Kong and Singapore in the Far East and the Falklands at the tip of South America. These were vital fuelling stations, providing the coal for steam powered ships. Britain also controlled the Cape Route around the tip of Africa to India and China. The explorer John Franklin made three daring attempts to find a Northwest Passage to India, which would have been shorter than the Cape Route. This route went past Greenland and over North America through the ice, but he never returned from his last attempt to find it.

Exporting the British Way of Life
The new colonies created jobs for British administrators, diplomats, engineers, surveyors, architects, traders, soldiers and people seeking to escape famine or poverty. They built railways, roads, bridges, factories and government buildings, all in the Victorian style and brought the British lifestyle and language to the world.

Did You Know?
Sepoys had to bite the ends off the cartridges they fired from their rifles. The cartridges were greased with animal fat, which was against the Hindu and Muslim religion. Even though the Indian government ordered that no cow or pig fat should be used, the sepoys did not believe it and they mutinied in 1857.

The Scramble for Africa
In the 1870's the only continent left to establish new colonies in was Africa and a 'scramble for Africa' began. Britain beat countries like Germany and France to gain the most land and Kenya, Uganda, Nigeria, southern Africa, Gambia, Sierra Leone and the Gold Coast became British colonies.

The White Man's Graveyard
Victorians who travelled to west Africa often died of malaria. The cure was quinine, but this came from the bark of a tree found in Spanish-controlled South America. The British continued to die from malaria. Then in 1859 a British explorer called Richard Spruce managed to collect enough plants and seeds to transport to India, where they were grown to produce quinine for British travellers.

Missionaries and Explorers
The expanding Empire offered lots of opportunity for explorers to discover new regions and to preach Christianity to the natives. Perhaps the most famous explorer was the Scottish doctor and scientist David Livingstone. An ordained missionary, he travelled to Africa and discovered the 350 foot high waterfall on the Zambezi River, which he named the Victoria Falls, after the Queen. He was proclaimed a hero in Britain. After several years an American journalist, Henry Morton Stanley, was sent by his newspaper to find Livingstone. When he found him Stanley raised his hat and famously said, "Dr Livingstone, I presume?" Stanley tried to persuade Livingstone to return to England, but Livingstone was obsessed with finding the source of the River Nile. He died in Africa in 1873 aged 60 and the Nile's source was eventually found by an army officer, John Hanning Speke.

HMS Warrior

HMS Warrior was the world's first iron-hulled armoured battleship. In 1860, when she was launched, she instantly made all other warships around the world obsolete. Her guns had a longer range and her combination of steam engines and sails made her faster than any other warship. Her iron armour made her stronger when under attack from enemy vessels. She could attack at a longer range than her opponents and anything she could not outgun she could outrun. However, during her short career with the Royal Navy not one shot was ever fired in anger. Today, you can see HMS Warrior at Portsmouth Historic Dockyard.

Mary Kingsley

Mary Kingsley was another intrepid explorer travelling alone in unexplored parts of west Africa. She climbed Mount Cameroon, which is over 4,000 metres high. She died of typhoid at the age of 38 years, whilst looking after wounded Boer War troops in Cape Town.

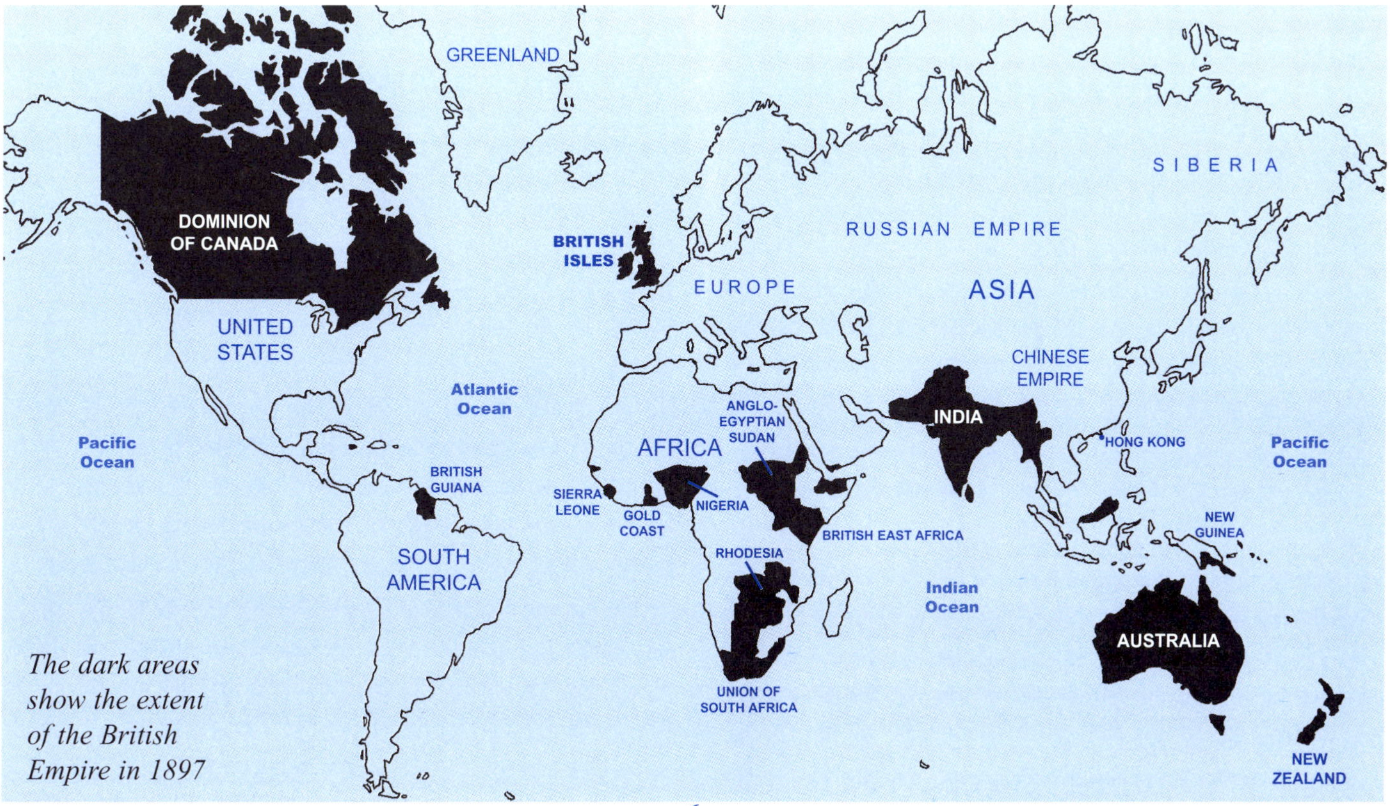

The dark areas show the extent of the British Empire in 1897

THE EMPIRE AT WAR

As Britain's Empire expanded wars were an inevitable result. Rising unemployment in Britain meant that there was no shortage of army recruits. Due to the invention of photography, the true horrors of these conflicts were brought home to the British public for the first time.

The Crimean War 1854-1856
The Crimean War was fought to stop Russian expansion into Turkish lands. The Russians felt that the Muslim Turks had been unfair to Christians in their Balkan territories, especially about access to holy places in Palestine. They also wanted to sail their ships through the Black Sea. British, French, Turkish and Sardinian forces landed at the Russian fortress of Sevastopol in the Crimea above the Black Sea. Although Russia was defeated, the British forces were not properly prepared, badly supplied and poorly led.

The 'Lady of the Lamp'
During the Crimean War, W H Russell who was a Times reporter, wrote about the awful conditions British wounded soldiers suffered in their military hospitals. Nurse Florence Nightingale was determined to do something about this and travelled to the region with 38 nurses. She was shocked by the hospital she visited. For every soldier who died of his wounds, seven were dying of disease due to the lack of proper sanitation, food, medical supplies and cleanliness. A total of 22,000 British troops died in the war, many from preventable diseases. She returned to England arguing fiercely for changes to be made to hospital conditions. She spent the remainder of her life training nurses and reforming hospitals until she died in 1910 at the age of 90.

The Victoria Cross
Queen Victoria took an interest in the lives of ordinary soldiers. She personally awarded medals to soldiers of all ranks and following her wishes, the Victoria Cross was created for outstanding bravery.

> **Did You Know?**
> The Victoria Cross is still made from the bronze of captured Russian cannons from the Crimean War. There is only a small amount left, however today the medal is not awarded as frequently as it was in previous conflicts.

Mary Seacole 1805-1881
Mary Seacole was the daughter of a Jamaican woman who ran a boarding house for soldiers and sailors. Her father was a Scottish soldier who had been posted to Jamaica. Mary became concerned about the fate of soldiers she had known in Jamaica, who were now serving in the Crimea. Although she wanted to help Florence Nightingale, she was told that no more nurses were needed, so she went to the Crimea alone. Mary set up a hotel and tended to the needs of the wounded. Unlike Florence's hospitals, which were 3 days sailing away from the Crimea, Mary was often seen bravely helping the wounded in the heat of battle. She was honoured at the end of the war for her bravery.

The Boer War 1899-1902
The Boers were South African farmers descended from Dutch settlers. They asked Britain to help them fight an army of 40,000 Zulus who threatened the Transvaal. In 1879 a local British force was massacred by Zulus, but reinforcements eventually put down the uprising. Britain then attempted to gain control of South Africa after the discovery of gold there. Using guerrilla tactics the Boers fought fiercely against the British in a vicious war. They were only defeated in the end by the much larger British army.

Maoris, Jamaicans, Russians and Chinese!
In New Zealand the British promised to protect Maori lands and when Europeans began settling there, war broke out. The British army also fought Jamaicans in the Caribbean, Russian advances into Afghanistan, which threatened India, as well as two Opium wars against the Chinese! The first Opium war began when the Chinese seized opium belonging to British merchants at Canton. The war ended with the Chinese agreeing to give Hong Kong to Britain.

The Crimean War

The Battle of Balaclava 1854
Tennyson's poem 'The Charge of the Light Brigade' was recited in every city, town and village in Britain. It appealed to Victorian patriotism, but the actual charge was a disaster. Russian cavalry had launched an attack on the British base at Balaclava in the Crimea. It was bravely defended by a handful of Highlander soldiers. Although heavily outnumbered the British heavy cavalry charged the Russian cavalry and forced them to retreat, but two of the British commanders at the battle were not on speaking terms and did not pursue the Russians to secure a victory. Worse was to follow. An order to protect British artillery was mistaken as an order to charge the Russian artillery! This resulted in the infamous charge of the Light Brigade. Out of 673 men amazingly only 113 were killed and 134 were wounded, but 517 horses died.

The British 'Tommy'
By the time of the Boer War British soldiers, or 'Tommy's', wore khaki uniforms. The word 'khaki' comes from a Hindustani word for 'dust'. Now they were better camouflaged than when they wore bright red uniforms. They had more accurate breech-loading rifles and smokeless powder in their cartridges. This meant that soldiers no longer gave their position away when firing their rifles. They also had machine guns, which could fire 300 rounds per minute, so a tiny force could defeat a vastly superior army.

Florence Nightingale often recruited her nurses from the nuns who worked in slums, or women who had experience in treating epidemics. She designed their uniforms, which were a cross between a nursing nun's dress and a servant's outfit. Try designing your own nurse's uniform.

A WEALTHY NATION

The Victorians believed that Britain was at the centre of the world and perhaps they had good reason for their confidence! Since the Industrial Revolution a century before, Britain had become the world's most powerful and technologically advanced nation.

Towns such as Manchester, Leeds, Sheffield and Birmingham grew into major industrial centres. Victorian businessmen and inventors made vast fortunes out of cotton, railways, coal and steel.

Iron and Steel
With the invention of the hot-blast furnace in 1828 coal could now be burnt instead of charcoal, making iron-working cheaper. James Nasmyth's steam-driven hammer of 1839 shaped iron with great precision. Henry Bessemer built a machine to convert iron into steel, which was much less brittle than cast iron. It made steel five thousand times faster than the best Sheffield steel! Steel was used to produce better artillery, as well as railway lines, bridges and ships.

Coal
Coal was used to power steam engines in locomotives, ships, factories and on farms. In 1890, 150 million tonnes of coal was mined, five times more than the amount mined when Victoria came to the throne 40 years before!

Farming
Mechanisation came to farming with steam-powered threshing machines and ploughs. There were riots by farm workers who lost their jobs, but eventually many of them left to work in the new industrial towns.

Cotton
Cotton became Britain's leading industry and at one time there were thousands of mills in Lancashire alone. Mills had been powered by water, but they were now being driven by steam engines and there was no longer a need to build factories near a river. Each machine was driven by a moving belt connected to overhead shafting driven by the steam engine. Other machinery could also be driven by belts powered by one steam engine. The 56 kilometre Manchester ship canal joined the city to the sea. This enabled American cotton to be imported and British cloth to be exported more quickly and efficiently.

Railways
Railways boosted the economy as they could take goods around the country faster. By 1870 there were almost 21,000 km of railway track and a train could travel at speeds of up to 95 kph.

Isambard Kingdom Brunel 1806-1859
The greatest railway builder and engineer was Brunel. At the age of 27 he won the job of building Britain's biggest railway, the Great Western Railway. For the first time a businessman could travel from Bristol to London and back in the same day. He also built the world's biggest ship of the time, the 'Great Eastern'. It was five times bigger than any other ship and took several weeks to launch sideways from a shipyard in Millwall. It rolled terribly and was never used to carry the 4,000 passengers it was designed for. Instead it laid telegraph cables across the Atlantic Ocean.

The world's first underground train on the Metropolitan line in London

🐾 Did You Know?
Unless you travelled first class you were likely to get wet, or were coated in soot, or fiery fragments from the train, as second class carriages did not have a roof! There were no toilets on the Bristol to London train, which was a four hour journey and it is said that people relieved themselves at the Swindon stop. The men walked to one end of the platform and the women went to the other end, both pretending to admire the view!

The Great Exhibition 1851

Queen Victoria opened the Great Exhibition in Hyde Park to show off the best of British art and design. It was a great success, with a quarter of Britain's population visiting it. Over 100,000 objects from around the world were displayed from furniture to steam trains, artificial limbs to rhubarb champagne.

Proceeds from the exhibition at the 'Crystal Palace' were used to open several large museums in London, including the Victoria and Albert, Science and Natural History Museums. The Palace was the first large public building to have toilets. The urinals were free, but you had to 'spend a penny' to use the cubicles.

The building was designed by Joseph Paxton and was six times the size of St Paul's Cathedral. It was made in Birmingham from pre-fabricated iron and glass parts, so that it could be dismantled and re-erected in Sydenham three years later. It survived there until it burned down in 1936.

If you were to hold a 'Great Exhibition' today, what kind of British products would you display? What things from around the world would you include to show off other countries?

Left, a worker at an Arkwright Water Frame (a spinning machine). It is the only one of its kind left in the world and is sited at **Helmshore Textile Museum** in the Rossendale Valley, Lancashire. Today, visitors can see machinery being operated and a working water wheel.

The **Queen Street Mill** in Burnley was Europe's last commercial steam powered weaving shed. Today, the steam engine 'Peace' is still in working order. During the Victorian period it powered 500 looms. The noise created by hundreds of looms was deafening and weavers could only communicate by lip reading, or sign language.

FAMILY LIFE

The Victorians took their lead from Queen Victoria and Prince Albert who enjoyed family life. Wealthier families could live the Victorian ideal, where the man was the head of the family and 'a woman's place was in the home'.

In a middle class, or wealthy family, the man was the provider and his word was never questioned. Until 1882 a married woman and anything she owned was considered to be her husband's property and she was not expected to work.

A Cluttered Home
A middle class home might seem cluttered and over-decorated by today's standards. Rooms were full of china, glass ornaments, paintings, patterned wallpaper, rugs and velvet upholstered furniture.

Pastimes
Families spent many hours in the drawing room where they 'withdrew' after dinner to talk, or receive guests. All respectable young women learned to play the piano and no Victorian drawing room was complete without one. The men would sing sentimental songs, or read a popular novel to everyone. Other pastimes included card games, such as Happy Families and board games like Ludo. Women enjoyed embroidery and cross-stitch.

> **Look at the houses where you live or near to your school. When were they built and were they made for working, middle or upper class families? If there is a Victorian house near you, or you live in one, how has it changed over the years? Is there a date plaque in the brickwork?**

Religion in the Home
At the beginning of Victoria's reign, 60% of the population went to church. In the evenings the father would read aloud from the Bible. Christmas became an important family occasion and it was Prince Albert who made it popular to have a decorated Christmas tree in the home and presents. Christmas cards appeared for the first time in 1846.

Children
Families were quite large, sometimes with as many as ten children, although not all would survive into adulthood. Children were brought-up strictly and were expected to be 'seen and not heard'. They were often looked after by nannies in the nursery before they reached school age. The nursery was full of toys such as dolls' houses, spinning tops, rocking horses, tin soldiers and lots of books. Clockwork toys and toy theatres were popular.

Servants
No upper or middle class family could survive without servants. They were summoned using bell pulls in the main rooms, which were connected by wires to bells in the kitchen. Most servants were women. Their work was hard, as there was no running hot water, washing machines, or vacuum cleaners. They were not paid very well and were given half a day off on a Sunday, one whole day off a month and two weeks holiday each year. Wealthy households employed a housekeeper, who was in charge of the female servants. The butler was in overall charge and the male servants answered to him. All of the servants ate together in the kitchen.

A Typical Day
A maid would rise early at around 6 a.m. and clean the large coal-fired iron 'range' used for cooking. She swept out the ashes, brushed, black-leaded and polished every part of the range and grates, then laid the coals and lit them. She had to light fires, set the tables, empty the smelly bedroom chamber pots, scrub the front steps and sometimes the pavement, polish boots and change the beds. There were ornaments to be dusted, carpets to beat and knives to polish. She would go to bed exhausted after 10 p.m. at night.

> **Did You Know?**
> Some people covered up the legs on their piano because they thought it was rude to leave them bare-legged!

Victorian Fashion

Women wore crinoline dresses over a wire cage to make them fan out, but by 1870 this was replaced by the bustle. By 1890 the bustle had disappeared and dresses were less full. The invention of the sewing machine meant that dresses and shoes became more daring in design. Ladies wore corsets of steel, bone or wood to give them tiny waists. They were so tight that they sometimes caused fainting. As with men, hats were always worn outside. Hairstyles were very elaborate, often incorporating wigs or false hair pieces.

Men wore frock coats, winged collars and spats, which were cloth gaiters over their shoes to protect them from mud. They also wore bow ties, ties with tie pins and waistcoats. They carried canes and wore pocket watches with chains.

Children were dressed formally in adult styles. Up to the age of five boys wore dresses like the girls! On Sundays everyone wore their best clothes to attend church.

A middle class family. The woman is wearing a crinoline dress

Above, a late Victorian dress

The Home

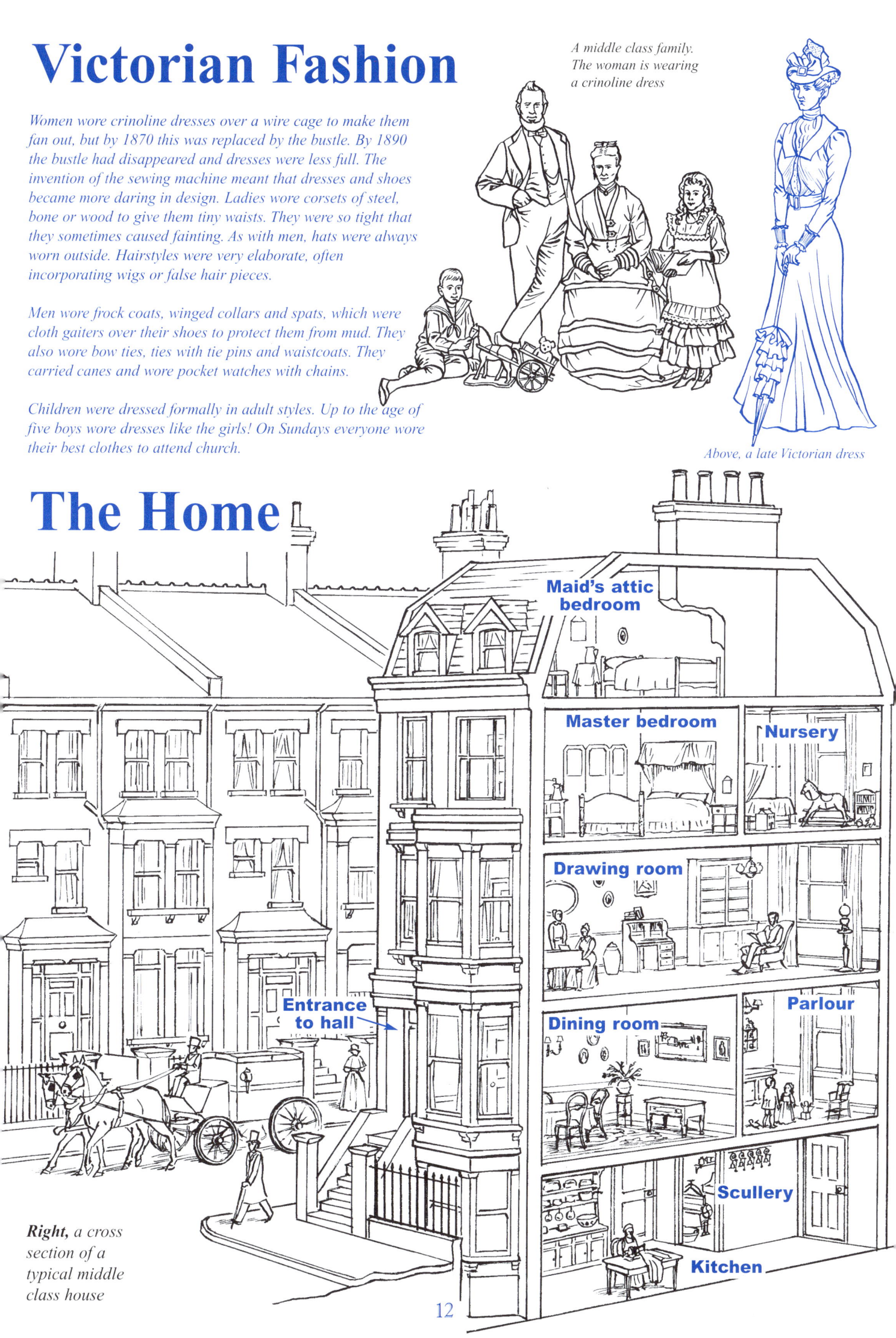

Right, *a cross section of a typical middle class house*

THE POOR

Although Britain was at the height of her wealth and power, the working classes lived in appalling conditions and worked up to eighteen hours a day. Hoping to escape the poverty many emigrated to Australia, America and Canada.

Factories
Most of the poor moved to towns to find work in the factories. Gradually a skilled labour force of shipbuilders, boiler-makers, engineers, miners and railway workers emerged, alongside the 'unskilled' labourers, such as dockers and chain makers. They lived in rows of poorly made 'back to back' terraced houses, which were erected near the factories. They did not own the house, but they paid rent to a landlord. They had to share a communal toilet, which was normally a shed over a hole in the ground. It was treated with quicklime to dissolve the waste. There were no drains, so slops were emptied into open gullies in the streets. As a result diarrhoea and fatal diseases like cholera and typhoid spread rapidly, while smoke from the factories polluted the air.

Workhouses and the Homeless
There were many homeless people who lived in overcrowded, unpleasant workhouses, where they were given a meal and a bed for a day's work. Men were often employed to break stones and women and children undertook laundry. Charles Dickens, whose writings drew attention to the plight of the poor, wrote about the workhouse in his book 'Oliver Twist'. Those who lived on the streets, including children, often became drunkards, as alcohol was cheaper than clean drinking water.

Women
Poor women earned money by working in mills, but their wages were lower than a man's. After a tough day at work the women returned home to clean and care for their families. They worked in mines, along with their entire family, although after 1842 women and children were no longer allowed to do this. There was no benefit system in Victorian times and if a family fell on hard times they had to sell their possessions to survive. There was no pension system to help widows either, so some women worked at home as seamstresses.

Street Traders
Street traders sold food from hand carts. Children sold firewood, or matches and girls offered posies of cut flowers for sale. Boys might sell poultry, or provide a shoe shine.

Children
A quarter of the labour force in Britain were children. Every family member had to work, or do chores around the house, or even make items such as toys to sell at fairs. The children who worked in factories and mills were often treated harshly and beaten if they did not work hard enough. Many were badly injured, or killed in mechanical accidents, as they crawled under dangerous machines to oil them. However, they lived in better conditions than the children in workhouses and were educated and taught their craft under the guidance of an experienced worker. Other children worked in the coal mines from as young as four years old. The only place for children to play was in the street, which was polluted with slops and horse dung. Many children had no shoes.

Country Life
Living conditions in the countryside were better than in the towns, even though most people lived in simple one-roomed cottages. On average a town dweller lived to the age of 40, but country people often lived ten years longer. Like the factory workers, farm workers paid rent to a landlord, although others built simple 'squatters' cottages' on common land to avoid paying rent. Apart from those who lost their jobs due to mechanised farming, workers such as shepherds and cattle herders continued their lives unaffected by progress.

> **Imagine what life was like for a typical working class family in Victorian times. Look around your house and write down all the things you would have to do without. List all the extra chores you would have to do without the modern conveniences we take for granted today.**

The Working Class

A typical working class family was crammed into one room, which was used for bathing, cooking and sleeping. Water was obtained from a tap, or a well in the street. If you wanted a hot bath the water had to be heated on the range and all of the family shared the same water!

Below, *whole families, including women, worked in coal mines. Boys were employed to open the doors of the wagons, or to pick amongst the rubble to find pieces of coal.*

Mudlarks & Climbing Boys

'Mudlarks' were children who waded in the filthy, stinking mud of the River Thames looking for scrap metal, or lost valuables to sell. 'Climbing boys' worked for chimney sweeps. They had to climb up inside the narrow chimneys and clean out the soot. Some got stuck and died of suffocation, or were severely burned. Charles Kingsley wrote about their suffering in his novel, 'The Water Babies'.

THE GREAT STINK!

During the long hot summer of 1858, the smell from sewage in the River Thames was so bad that MP's in the newly built Houses of Parliament could not open the windows to let fresh air in. The 'Great Stink' was debated in Parliament and three million pounds was allocated to build sewers and pumping stations. After their construction by Sir Joseph Bazalgette, there were no more outbreaks of cholera and typhoid and no great stink! They were so well built that they are still in use today.

EDUCATION AND SOCIAL REFORM

At the beginning of Victoria's reign there was no official school system. Workers had few rights, trade unions were banned and only a few people could vote. By the end of her reign all of this had changed with the introduction of new laws and public services.

Education for the Poor
For poor children there were Sunday schools, or 'ragged schools', which provided free meals and clothing. There were church-run schools, which cost a few pennies a week. By 1870 a national system of schools was set up and funded by local taxes. However, attendance was limited because children had to work, or look after their younger brothers and sisters at home.

In 1880 the government made school compulsory for 5-10 year olds and this was later extended to 13 year olds. In 1891 a law made primary education free for all. Victorian education aimed to equip children for work, so they learned the 'three Rs', reading, writing and arithmetic. They were also taught geography, history, sport or 'drill' and read the Bible. Boys were taught woodwork, whilst girls learned to cook.

Education for the Rich
Wealthy boys went to public schools like Eton, Rugby or Westminster and learned Latin and Greek. They were educated to become leaders and statesmen. Girls from the age of 5 or 6 were taught mainly by governesses at home.

Chartism and Trade Unions
Members of Parliament, or MP's, represented the interests of landowners rather than the middle or working classes. In 1836 a People's Charter was presented to Parliament demanding the right to vote for all workers, secret ballots at elections, an end to MP's having to be landowners and other reforms. It was rejected, but most of its demands eventually became law. There were many Chartist demonstrations and in 1839, 24 people were killed in riots at Newport and Birmingham. Workers realised their importance and banded together to form trade unions to improve their pay and conditions. They could now put pressure on employers who needed their skills. Less skilled workers improved their lot by striking. In the 1870's trade unions were legalised.

Reforms for Workers
Many Acts of Parliament were passed to improve the lives of workers, such as the Factory Act in 1833. This banned children under 9 years old from working in factories and mills and stopped night work for the under 18's. In 1842 women and children under 10 years were banned from underground work in mines. Many women fought this law because they needed the money. Later laws restricted factory work for older children and women to ten hours a day.

Political Parties
The reforms were fought for in Parliament by the new political parties formed during this period. The three parties were the Conservative and Union Party, Liberal Party, which emerged in the 1850's and introduced the working class vote and the Independent Labour Party, begun in 1893.

Ireland
The Irish survived largely on a diet of potatoes. They grew other crops, but these went to enrich English landlords, many of whom lived in England. In 1845 and 1846 the potato crop was ruined by disease, which caused a million deaths from famine. The Corn Laws were repealed allowing cheap imports of corn from America, but this came too late to save people from starvation. One million Irish people chose to emigrate to America, travelling in appalling conditions in converted slave ships. Britain's lack of care during this terrible time increased Irish hatred towards the English.

Did You Know?
Some trade unions used extreme methods to encourage other workers to fall in line. It was not unknown for cutlery workers in Sheffield to drop a keg of gunpowder down the chimney of a fellow worker!

List all of the rights and privileges you enjoy, which ordinary working Victorians did not have. People lost their lives fighting and campaigning for better working and living conditions.

A Victorian School

Children learned by copying facts from a blackboard using a slate-pencil on a slate board. Older children had ink pens and copybooks. Teachers sometimes delegated the teaching to older pupils, or monitors, who were paid one shilling a week to teach the younger children. Discipline was strict. Teachers used bamboo canes, or leather straps to punish naughty pupils, or if they did not learn a lesson they were made to stand in a corner wearing a cone-shaped dunce's cap. Charles Dickens wrote about a 'horror-school' called Dotheboys Hall in his novel 'Nicholas Nickleby', where boys were very cruelly treated.

Lord Shaftesbury 1801-1885

Many Victorians were great philanthropists. Inspired by their religious beliefs of Christian charity, they built houses, public baths, libraries, parks and hospitals. Lord Shaftesbury devoted his life to the care of the underprivileged. He campaigned for better working conditions, more time off, set up 'ragged schools' and supported orphanages. He demanded that homes have clean water and proper sanitation. He championed the cause of 'climbing boys' (page 13) and campaigned for better care for the mentally insane. After he died thousands of poor people lined the streets at his memorial service in Westminster Abbey.

The Sally Army and Dr Barnardo's

William and Catherine Booth started the Salvation Army from their Whitechapel Christian Mission in London. They helped homeless people and alcoholics. Thomas and Syrie Barnardo opened children's homes in London for the homeless, particularly those with disabilities and learning difficulties.

William Hesketh Lever 1851-1925

Some factory and mill owners known as 'enlightened industrialists' were appalled at the conditions faced by most workers. They were determined to provide better quality housing, working conditions, education and welfare for their employees. One of the best examples is Port Sunlight created in 1888 by soap manufacturer William Hesketh Lever. Lever had a vision of people living and working in harmony with nature and industry and employed over 30 architects to make it a reality.

ART AND ENTERTAINMENT

Some of the most distinguished buildings in Britain date from the Victorian period. Beside the sentimental art and grand designs common at that time, there was also great creativity and innovation.

Architecture
The Victorians chose the medieval 'Gothic Revival' style for their architecture. Its solid, ornate, yet practical style satisfied their Christian values. They built magnificent buildings and bridges in brick, iron, steel and glass, such as the Houses of Parliament, St Pancras railway station in London and the Crystal Palace. The Forth Bridge across the Firth of Forth in Scotland was the largest bridge of its time.

Art
For the first time public art galleries opened so that people of all classes could enjoy art. Sentimental scenes from everyday life, poetry, the Bible, legends and medieval themes were popular. Paintings were of romantic ideals full of nature and often contained a strong moral message. Famous artists included Millais, Hunt and Rossetti who were members of the Pre-Raphaelite Brotherhood.

Literature
Public libraries and cheaper printing methods fuelled the thirst for books, magazines and comics. Literature was the television of the age. Charles Dickens was the most famous novelist and his work was serialised in magazines before being published in book form. Other famous writers included Bram Stoker, the Brontë sisters, Thomas Hardy, Rudyard Kipling, Robert Lewis Stephenson, Lewis Carrol and Arthur Conan Doyle, who created the fictional detective Sherlock Holmes.

Photography
William Henry Fox Talbot improved early photographic techniques to produce a more workable method. By the 1880's amateurs were using Kodak box cameras with roll film. People loved photography, in particular family portraits against a studio background. 'Carte-de-vistes' were popular 'visiting cards' with a photographic portrait on the back. When Prince Albert died 70,000 of his carte-de-vistes were sold in one week.

Holidays
By the second half of Victoria's reign working people had more time off and more spending money due to the various reforms. The middle classes took advantage of the expanding holiday industry. In the 1880's, Thomas Cook offered tourists trips to Europe, the Holy Land and the Egyptian pyramids.

Entertainment
At the theatre you could hear music by Mendelssohn, or Verdi. You could see Gilbert and Sullivan operas, ballet, serious plays and variety shows. For a few pennies you could go to a music hall and enjoy comedy, a sing-song, pantomimes and juggling. In the 1890's there were over 350 music halls in London alone, many of which started life as a room in a pub.

Outdoor Games
The wealthy played cricket. W. G. Grace, perhaps the most famous cricketer of all, once scored 224 not out. Lawn tennis began and the Wimbledon men's championships were first held in 1877. The Football Association was formed in 1863 and established national rules for the various clubs. It changed from a public school game to a working class pursuit and became a great spectator sport.

Charles Dickens 1812-1870
Dickens was born in Portsmouth, Hampshire, but his family moved to London when he was a boy. They were reasonably well-off until his father was imprisoned for falling into debt. After working in a factory and then in a law firm, Dickens eventually became a journalist. He wrote his first full novel, 'The Pickwick Papers', in the year Victoria came to the throne. It was an instant success. Dickens was a keen observer of all classes of people, from the poorest to the richest. He created some of the most famous characters in British literature, such as Ebenezer Scrooge from 'A Christmas Carol'. His well known works include 'Oliver Twist', 'Nicholas Nickleby', 'The Old Curiosity Shop', 'David Copperfield', 'Bleak House', 'A Tale of Two Cities' and 'Great Expectations'.

Victorian Style

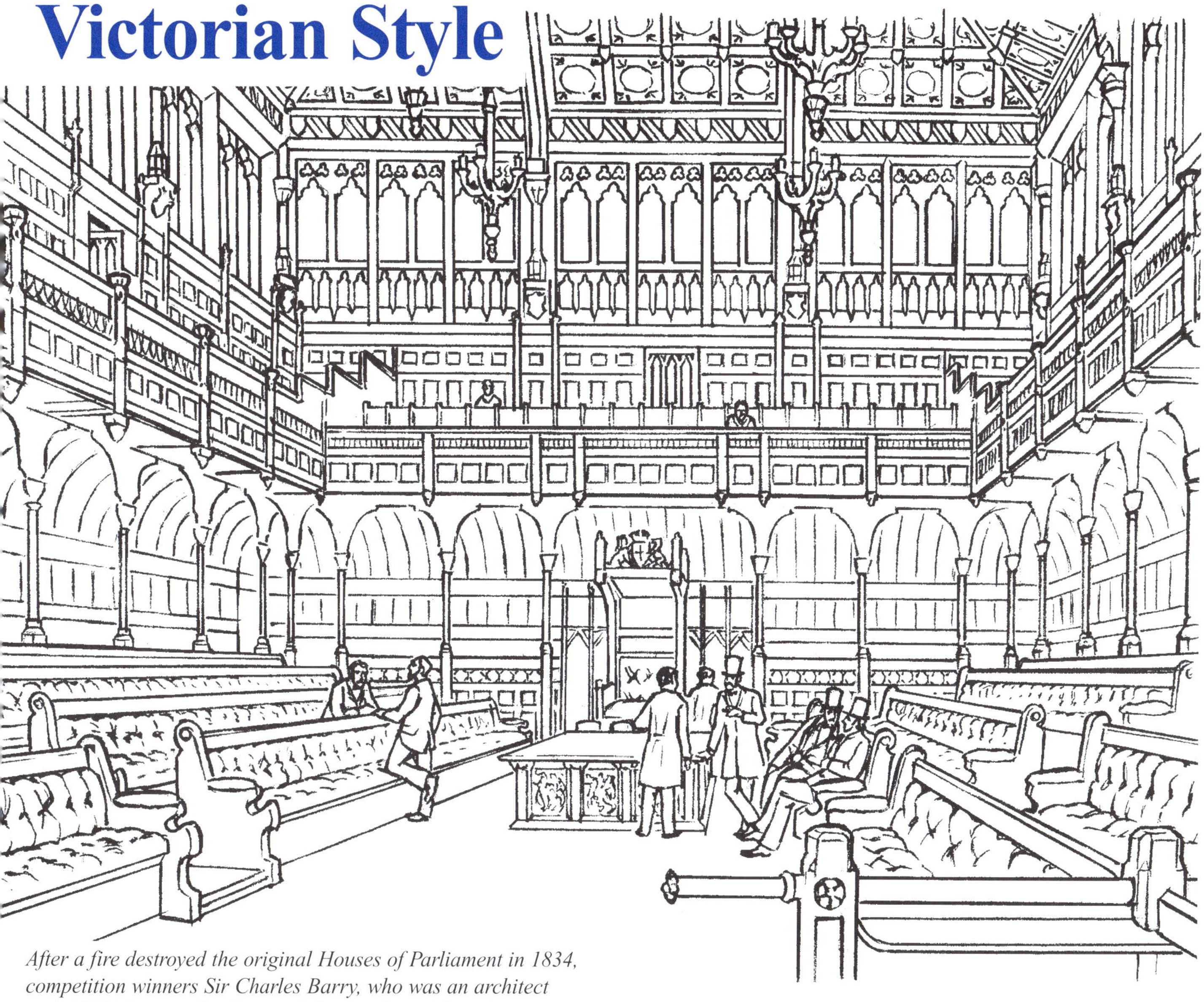

After a fire destroyed the original Houses of Parliament in 1834, competition winners Sir Charles Barry, who was an architect and A W N Pugin, who designed the details and furnishings, created together a new building in the Gothic Revival style.

Right, *a wallpaper design by William Morris (1834-1896). He was a leading artist and designer in the Arts and Crafts movement. This group of artists disliked mass production and too much ornamentation and they took their inspiration from the medieval period.*

Above, *this beautifully proportioned furniture was the work of Charles Rene Macintosh (1868-1928), a Scottish architect and designer who was a member of the Arts and Crafts movement.*

Did You Know?
Poor children used to make a football from a pig's bladder, bought from a butcher and blown up like a balloon!

Look at the list of authors on the left under 'Literature'. Find out what books they wrote and name some other well known Victorian writers.

Did You Know?
The novelist George Eliot (1819-1880) was actually a woman called Mary Ann Evans. She used a 'pen name' so that she would not be confused with female romantic writers. Her relationship with a married man would have been scandalous at the time. The Brontë sisters wrote under the pseudonyms Currer, Ellis and Acton Bell.

OUR VICTORIAN INHERITANCE

When Queen Victoria died in 1901, aged 81 her coffin was taken to London and put on a gun-carriage. Its journey through the city was seen by mourners all over the Empire. The Victorian era was over and Edward VII was to inherit a more uncertain future for Britain.

Britain Radically Changed
Victoria had been Britain's longest reigning monarch, during which time the country had completely changed. Once an agricultural economy, Britain was now a leading industrial power. Victorians made things to last and today we can still see their statues, railway stations, bridges, public libraries, government buildings, museums, schools and seaside piers.

Inventions
The Victorians gave us many things we now take for granted and here are just some of them. Public lavatories, which flushed and appeared in wealthy homes from the 1850's. The calculator was invented by Charles Babbage. The first man-powered flight by George Cayley was in 1853. The double-decker bus was first seen and then the world's first underground railway in 1863, on the Metropolitan line. It was steam powered, so the tunnels were very smoky, but in 1890 the first electric underground railway opened.

Other innovations included the bicycle, which by 1885 looked like a modern bike in its design. The pneumatic tyre was invented by a Scottish vet called John Boyd Dunlop. The electric tramcar was first seen in Blackpool. The submarine, self-propelled torpedoes, oil lamps and electric lights, invented over here by Joseph Swan at the same time as Edison in the US. Both inventors eventually formed a company together. Also tinned food and can openers appeared. The telephone was patented by Alexander Bell in 1876. The world's first hydro-electric power station opened in 1881 at Godalming in Surrey and provided electricity for street lighting and a few private homes. The cordless electric iron came in 1882 and the electric oven in 1891.

Discoveries
The naturalist Charles Darwin (1809-1882) developed his theory of evolution, mainly from observations of nature he made during his five year voyage around the world in HMS Beagle. His book 'On the Origin of Species by Means of Natural Selection' shocked the world, especially as Victorians believed the creation story in the Bible.

Medical Advances
Joseph Lister discovered disinfectants, which could be sprayed on wounds and instruments to kill bacteria, making them 'antiseptic' or germ free. The survival rate of patients during surgery doubled as a result of this. Sir James Simpson pioneered the use of anaesthetics in the 1840's. Previously operations had been carried out without the use of painkillers. Queen Victoria was given chloroform vapour during the birth of her eighth child. The arrival of the endoscope allowed doctors to look into a patients' body without having to cut it open.

The Post Office
Our postal service began in 1840 when Rowland Hill decided that people should pay in advance to send letters. He introduced the first postage stamp. Letter, or 'pillar' boxes followed 15 years later.

Read All About It!
After the removal of the tax on newspapers, cheaper 'penny' papers were printed in huge numbers. With the invention of the telegraph news stories from around the world could be reported in the press within a day. The cleverly named 'Daily Telegraph' had the highest circulation of all the daily newspapers.

Did You Know?
When Bell first demonstrated the telephone his first words were "Watson, come here, I want you!" Apparently he had spilt acid on his trousers and was summoning help!

Did You Know?
You might think that tea originally came from India, but in actual fact Chinese tea was introduced as a crop to India through the work of botanists at Kew Gardens in London.

Jack the Ripper

The most infamous criminal in Victorian times was Jack the Ripper, who murdered several prostitutes in the Whitechapel area of East London in 1888. Victims had their throats slashed and were horribly mutilated with a knife. A letter and postcard signed 'Jack the Ripper' were sent by the murderer to a news agency. Despite a police investigation, stake-outs and the use of bloodhounds no one was ever convicted of the crimes.

Crime and Punishment

There were so many homeless and poor people on the streets, particularly in the growing towns, that many turned to crime to survive. There were pickpockets, burglars and gangs of thieves wandering the streets at night looking for victims.

To combat this, the first British police force was created in London by Sir Robert Peel in 1829. They were modelled on the river police, who had been around much longer. They were originally equipped with a wooden truncheon, cutlass, handcuffs and wore a top hat. Before whistles came in 1880 they used a wooden rattle to summon help. Eventually most major towns had their own police force.

Prisons were so overcrowded that some prisoners were kept in 'hulks' moored on rivers. Until 1868 criminals could still be transported to the colonies. Murder and treason were punishable by hanging, but there were severe punishments for lesser crimes. Prisoners originally had to do pointless tasks, such as turning a crank handle 10,000 times in an eight-hour day. The wardens would sometimes turn a screw on the crank to make the job harder, so they earned the nickname 'screws'. When the Victorians realised that once prisoners were released they often re-offended, more useful tasks were given to the prisoners, such as sewing uniforms, or farming to help them to become good citizens when their sentences ended.

Police Equipment
a) cutlass b) handcuffs
c) truncheon d) rattle

🦅 Did You Know?
For stealing a bottle of ginger beer and some tobacco, two Portsmouth boys aged 13 and 15 were flogged and jailed for 12 months.

Design a Victorian newspaper and think of a name for it. Include stories of crimes, current events, tragic world news, such as wars and other items perhaps about the royal family. Add black and white illustrations too.

Giant Victorian Word Search

T	H	E	C	R	I	M	E	A	N	W	A	R	A	W	R	L	S	O	P
A	Q	N	E	B	S	O	D	R	A	N	R	A	B	R	D	E	J	E	R
T	N	Y	E	L	O	C	A	E	S	Y	R	A	M	Y	S	A	L	H	B
T	G	U	V	E	S	T	E	E	L	V	S	A	A	R	C	A	U	N	U
L	R	A	S	I	U	Q	S	A	M	E	R	I	E	K	G	R	D	E	C
E	E	L	B	C	C	U	S	N	S	Y	U	T	T	N	C	S	C	L	K
A	A	H	R	N	A	T	X	U	K	R	S	H	I	H	N	P	H	T	I
I	T	U	U	M	S	V	O	I	T	I	E	T	M	E	T	R	A	S	N
R	E	T	N	N	G	H	N	R	S	R	H	S	K	P	O	I	R	A	G
O	X	T	E	D	K	G	A	E	I	G	W	C	R	P	C	N	L	C	H
T	H	O	L	R	S	T	T	P	I	A	I	I	I	I	O	C	E	R	A
C	I	N	O	L	S	N	P	N	R	D	C	S	R	O	A	E	S	O	M
I	B	W	E	E	O	E	E	R	S	C	Q	R	T	M	L	A	D	S	P
V	I	Y	T	R	R	C	I	E	E	L	D	S	O	R	L	L	A	D	A
N	T	O	B	H	N	O	L	X	O	O	E	C	E	S	Y	B	R	N	L
E	I	S	K	E	R	R	L	U	P	I	A	N	O	S	S	E	W	I	A
E	O	I	R	A	A	B	A	M	N	O	T	T	O	C	U	R	I	W	C
U	N	O	O	H	M	Y	M	U	D	L	A	R	K	S	S	T	N	T	E
Q	L	S	C	R	I	N	O	L	I	N	E	D	R	E	S	S	T	A	C
F	E	S	T	Y	R	U	B	S	E	T	F	A	H	S	D	R	O	L	Z

Queen Victoria HMS Warrior Coal Workhouses Brunel
Prince Albert Victoria Cross Cotton Dr Barnardos Great Exhibition
Windsor Castle The Crimean War Steel Bronte Sisters Crinoline Dress
Buckingham Palace Florence Nightingale Charles Dickens Lord Shaftesbury Jack the Ripper
Mary Kingsley Mary Seacole Mudlarks Piano Charles Darwin

Please return this book on or before the date shown above. To renew go to www.essex.gov.uk/libraries, ring 0345 603 7628 or go to any Essex library.

Essex County Council

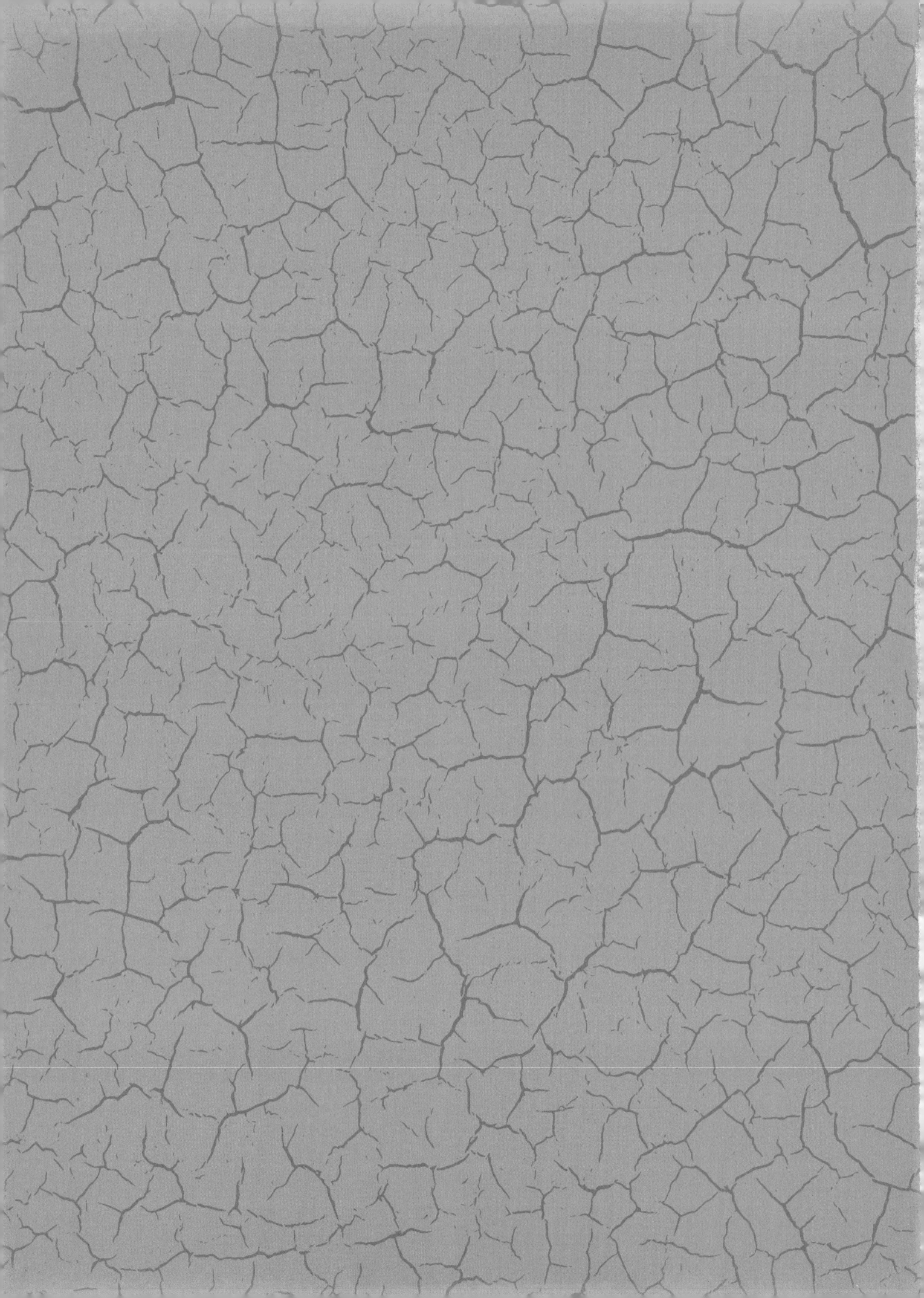

Hot Planet

HOW CLIMATE CHANGE IS HARMING OUR WORLD

(AND WHAT YOU CAN DO TO HELP)

ANNA CLAYBOURNE

FRANKLIN WATTS
LONDON · SYDNEY

Franklin Watts
First published in Great Britain in 2020 by the Watts Publishing Group
Copyright © the Watts Publishing Group 2020

All rights reserved.

Editor: Julia Bird
Designer: Rocket Design (East Anglia) Ltd

Picture credits:
Alamy: Hilary Morgan 12b; Prisma Archivo 8c.
Getty Images: AFP 13bl; Ted Aljibe/AFP/ 28b; Anterra/UIG 18bl; Bloomberg 38t; Peter Cade 13c; Yasuyoshi Chiba 37c; Christophel Fine Arts/UIG 12cl; Nur Photo 16bl; Jeremie Richard/AFP 21b; Michael Tewelde 31b; Universal Images 28t.
Laboratory for Nanobioelectronics, US San Diego Jacobs School of Engineering: 41t.
N Lazarnick/DPL/PD: 9cr.
NASA:The Earth Observatory 21t, 21c.
NMUSAF/US Air Force photo: 12cr.
Science Photo Library: Mark Thomas 40t.
Shutterstock: A78805 23b; Aisyaqilumaranas 39t; AnaitSmi 11cr; Anatolia 15bl; Andrey-1/S 41c; AnnstasAg 22bl; ArdeaA 3tl, 3br, 4-5c, 11b, 14-15bg, 30-31bg, 32-33bg, 32c, 38-39bg, 40b, 43b; arka38 24bl; Breedfoto 37tl; Juan Carita/AP/REX 14b; Chalintra B 38bl; chrupka 20c; Clenpies Design 9t, 39b; Dmitry375 22tr; Domicoolka 7b; Droid-worker 19b; ecco 12-13bg; Everilda 15br; Frank60 26c; freesoulproduction 14cr;Gaidamashchuk 15c; Giamportone 33cl; Golden Sikorka 34tc; GoodStock 17b; GoodStudio 2, 6-7c, 26b; GraficsRF 17cl, 25cl; Hennadi H 23tl; Sutton Hibert/REX 27t; ieronim 22br; Incomibile 25cr; Semiankova Inha 22tl; KNO 16c; Yevgen Kravchenko 1c;Lemburg Vector Studio 20-21bg; Mikko Lemola 43t; light s 33cr; macrovector 5br;CL-Medien 13t; MicroOne 3tr, 10cl, 13br, 33t, 35b; mything 15bc; Roman Nerud 9cl;Peter Niesen 24br; Oakview Studios 35c; Oceloti 8-9bg; Oleg7799 25bl; petogarva 10tl, 31tl, 36; Pixsooz 27br; Pol9334 10b; Pyty 20t; Qualit Design 42b; Robuart 18t, 34b; Roi and Roi 38b;Andrew Rybalko 3bl, 4bl; Sensvector 34tc; Shanvood 23tr; Stu Shaw 42t; Silken Photography 19t; Amanita Silvicora 18-19b; SkyPics Studio 10tr; Slowga 25br; Natali Snailcat 24-25bg; Sunny Dream 10cr; Sunshine Vector 17cl, 17cr; Mascha Tace 31tr; Tarikdiz 29; Tuaklom 27c;Vasosh 24t; venimo 37b; vidkont 1bg; Warxar 38br; Richard Whitcombe 25t; Chamille White 9cl; Mei Yanotai 10tc.

Every effort has been made to clear copyright. Should there be any inadvertent omission, please apply to the publisher for rectification.

ISBN: 978 1 4451 6988 0

Printed in Dubai

Franklin Watts
An imprint of
Hachette Children's Group
Part of the Watts Publishing Group
Carmelite House
50 Victoria Embankment
London EC4Y 0DZ

An Hachette UK Company
www.hachette.co.uk
www.franklinwatts.co.uk

Contents

The heat is on 4
Greenhouse Earth 6
How it happened 8
Carbon dioxide 10
CASE STUDY: Air travel 12
Farming and warming 14
Changing the weather 16
Melting ice 18
CASE STUDY: Okjökull glacier 20
Impact on wildlife 22
CASE STUDY: The Great Barrier Reef ... 24
Impact on humans 26
CASE STUDY: Super Typhoon Haiyan ... 28
What can the world do? 30
What can you do? 32
Transport revolution 34
Power sources 36
Future farming 38
Science solutions 40
A cooler future? 42
Glossary 44
Further information 46
Index 48

THE HEAT IS ON

There is a huge problem facing our planet, the Earth. It's getting hotter and hotter, and this could have disastrous results. We call this global warming. 'Warming' sounds quite nice, like a sunny summer's day. In fact, Earth isn't just warming – it's overheating.

THE CHANGING CLIMATE

'Climate' means average weather patterns and temperatures. Earth's climate has always changed naturally. For example, when the dinosaur *Tyrannosaurus rex* was alive, it was several degrees hotter than it is now. And 20,000 years ago, during the last ice age, it was colder.

But this time it's different. Why?

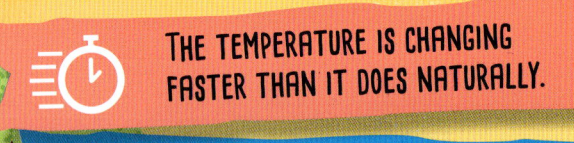

- The temperature is changing faster than it does naturally.
- This time, human activities are the cause.

The main cause of recent global warming is burning fuel - for example in cars, factories and power stations. It releases gases into the air that make the Earth heat up.

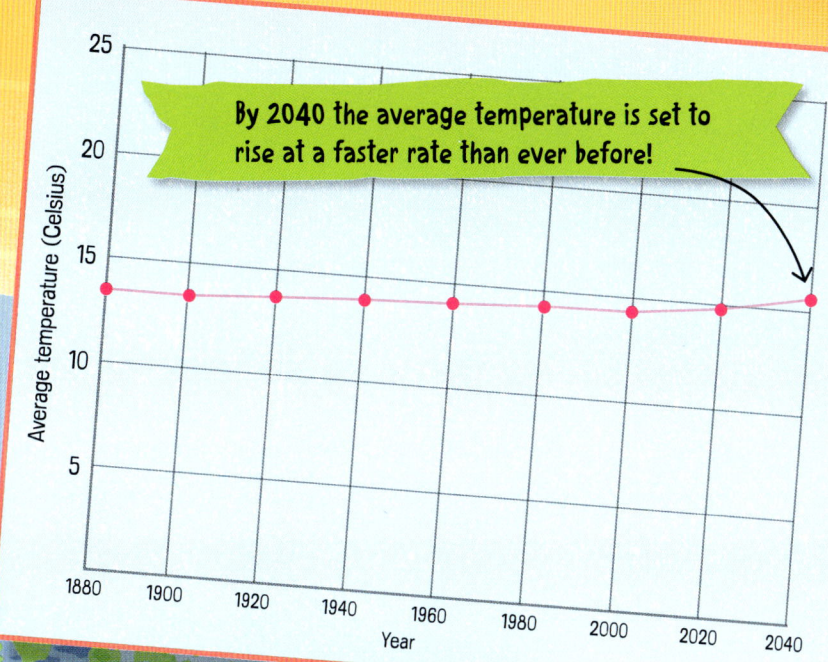

By 2040 the average temperature is set to rise at a faster rate than ever before!

GOING UP!

Since the year 1880, the Earth's average temperature has gone up by almost 1 degree Celsius. That might not sound like much, but it is. The Earth's climate is delicately balanced, and a 1°C change has a big impact.

CLIMATE EMERGENCY

Global warming doesn't just cause hotter weather. It has many different effects, which are already being seen all around the world.

Polar ice melts and sea levels rise.

There are bigger, more dangerous wildfires and storms.

Some places get more rain and floods, while others have more droughts.

We caused this problem, and we need to find a solution – fast. This book explores how it happened, and what we can do.

GREENHOUSE EARTH

How can some gases in the air make the world warmer? It happens because of the greenhouse effect. A few types of gas, known as greenhouse gases, cause the greenhouse effect by trapping heat from the Sun close to the Earth.

WHY GREENHOUSE?

It's called the greenhouse effect because it works like a greenhouse! A greenhouse is made of glass, which lets in the Sun's light energy, warming up the inside. But the glass also stops most of the heat from escaping, so the inside of the greenhouse stays warm.

The Earth's atmosphere does the same thing. Sunlight shines through it and warms the Earth. The air around the Earth warms up too. But gases in the air stop some of this heat from escaping back out into space, keeping the Earth's surface warm.

NOT ALL BAD

The greenhouse effect isn't a bad thing in itself. It's a natural process that keeps the Earth warm enough to live on. Without it, the average temperature would be a f-f-f-freezing −18°C!

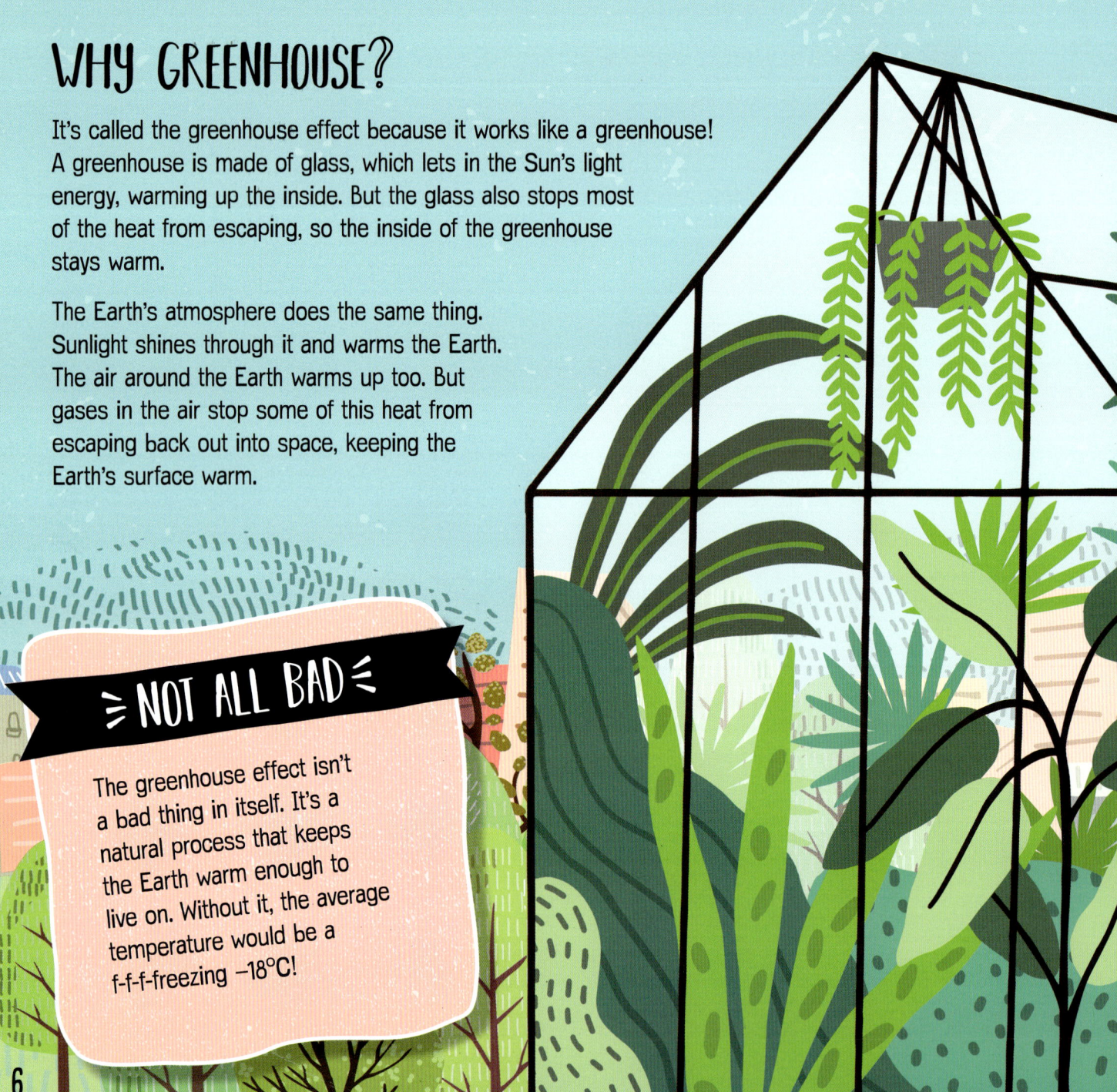

GUIDE TO GREENHOUSE GASES

The problem starts when we add more greenhouse gases, making the Earth *too* warm. So which gases are they? Here's a handy guide:

76%
CARBON DIOXIDE (CO_2)
Makes up about 3/4 of the greenhouse gases we release. Mainly comes from burning fuel, such as coal, gas, oil and wood.

16%
METHANE
Mainly comes from farm animals, and extracting fossil fuels.

6%
NITROUS OXIDE
From burning fuel, and from some farm and factory chemicals.

2%
OTHER GASES
There are several other greenhouse gases, such as hydrofluorocarbons, which are used in fridges.

As cows digest their food, they burp and fart out methane gas. One dairy cow can release up to 700 litres of methane a day - enough to fill 50 party balloons!

HOW IT HAPPENED

Long ago, human-made global warming wasn't a problem. It became an issue because of huge changes in society that began in the 18th century. These changes became known as the Industrial Revolution (1760–1840), and led to a big increase in greenhouse gases.

FACTORIES

People began working in big factories, using newly-invented machines to make things - instead of making things in their homes or local workshops.

INVENTIONS AND IDEAS

Throughout history, humans have come up with new technology and ideas. During the Industrial Revolution, a number of important inventions changed the way most people lived and worked. Here are some of the main ones...

1750

MORE PEOPLE

These inventions and discoveries began to make many people wealthier and healthier. More people were born, more of them lived longer and the world's population grew faster and faster.

THE WORLD'S POPULATION IS NOW MORE THAN EIGHT TIMES WHAT IT WAS BEFORE THE INDUSTRIAL REVOLUTION!

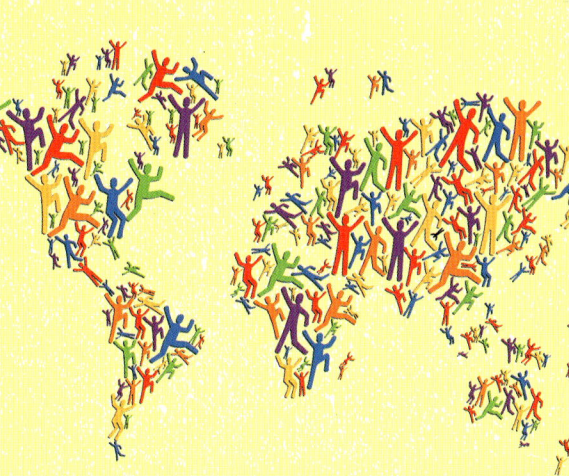

MEDICINES

New medical discoveries, such as vaccinations and germ-killing chemicals, saved millions of lives.

ELECTRICITY

We discovered more about how electricity worked, and used it to power machines and gadgets, such as light bulbs.

1850

1800

ENGINES

We invented steam and combustion engines, which burned fuel to power factory machines, and led to other inventions, like trains and cars.

1900

CRAZY WORLD

Lots more people meant we needed more food and clothes, and more farms and factories to supply them. Trains and cars meant we could travel to work and go on holiday. Cities became bigger and busier. Houses were linked up to electricity, and we invented more electrical gadgets.

And that's how we ended up here – burning loads of fuel, using loads of energy and taking up huge areas of land for cities, farms, factories and roads.

CARBON DIOXIDE

The most important greenhouse gas is carbon dioxide, also known by its chemical symbol CO_2. We pour billions of tonnes of it into the atmosphere every year by burning fuels to release useful energy – especially fossil fuels like coal, oil and gas.

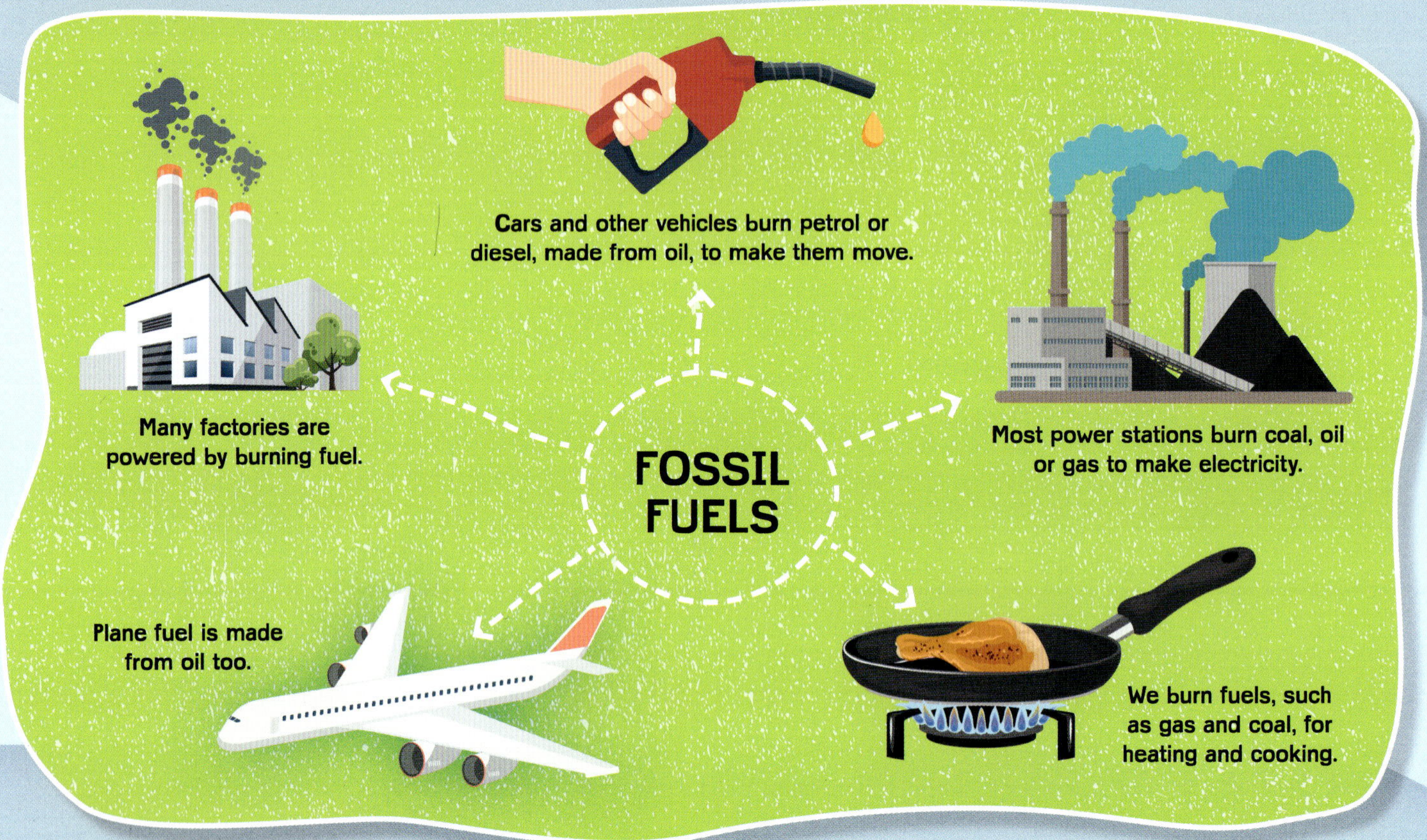

FOSSIL FUELS

Many factories are powered by burning fuel.

Cars and other vehicles burn petrol or diesel, made from oil, to make them move.

Most power stations burn coal, oil or gas to make electricity.

Plane fuel is made from oil too.

We burn fuels, such as gas and coal, for heating and cooking.

HOW IT WORKS

Most fuel comes from living things. For example, coal, oil and gas formed in prehistoric times from the remains of dead plants and animals. (That's why they're called fossil fuels!) Wood from trees is also used as fuel.

Living things contain the element carbon. When fuel made from living things burns, the carbon reacts with oxygen in the air, and this creates carbon dioxide gas.

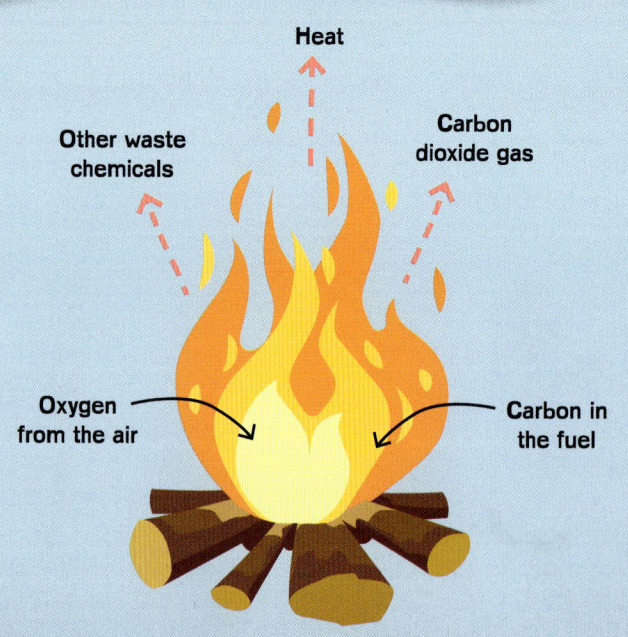

Heat · Other waste chemicals · Carbon dioxide gas · Oxygen from the air · Carbon in the fuel

10

STORED CARBON

There's a lot of carbon on our planet. Some of it floats around in carbon dioxide gas, but most of it is locked away in rocks and soil, dissolved in the sea, and stored in living things, especially plants.

The more plant matter there is, the more carbon is kept locked up, instead of being turned into carbon dioxide and acting as a greenhouse gas.

SOME OTHER HUMAN ACTIVITIES ALSO EMIT CARBON DIOXIDE, SUCH AS MAKING CONCRETE TO USE FOR BUILDING.

KEEPING COUNT

Scientists measure the carbon dioxide in the atmosphere in parts per million (ppm). For most of human history, it's been below 300 ppm – but since 1800, it's risen to over 415 ppm.

CASE STUDY
AIR TRAVEL

A hundred years ago, hardly anyone had been on an aeroplane. Today, you probably have, and so have many of your family and friends. But all this flying contributes to global warming, as planes release a LOT of greenhouse gas.

HOW FLYING TOOK OFF

Humans have been flying since 1783, when brothers Joseph-Michel and Jacques-Étienne Montgolfier built the first passenger-carrying hot air balloon. It was the start of a love affair with the air...

JET FLIGHT
THE FIRST JET AIRCRAFT TO FLY WAS THE HEINKEL HE 178.

1939

1903

1783

POWERED FLIGHT
THE WRIGHT BROTHERS MAKE THE FIRST POWERED AIRCRAFT FLIGHTS IN THEIR ENGINE-DRIVEN PLANE, THE *WRIGHT FLYER*.

HOT AIR BALLOON
THE MONTGOLFIER BROTHERS LAUNCH THE FIRST HOT AIR BALLOON FLIGHT.

At any given moment, there are around 10,000 planes in the air...
...carrying over 1 million passengers...
...and there are over 4 billion individual passenger flights a year.

JETTING OFF

Flying is normal for many people around the world.

TODAY

JUMBO!

Launch of the Boeing 747 jumbo jet.

1970

1952

JET AIRLINER

Launch of the first commercial jet airliner, the De Havilland Comet.

≽ PLANES AND THE PLANET ≼

Planes aren't the biggest cause of greenhouse gases, but they're still a problem. They emit more greenhouse gas per passenger, per kilometre, than trains, buses or cars. They release these gases high in the atmosphere, where they have a stronger greenhouse effect. And cheap flights encourage us to travel much longer distances than we would if they weren't an option.

Even worse, despite climate change, people are flying more and more, not less.

FARMING AND WARMING

Agriculture, or farming, is a big cause of global warming too. Farms release greenhouse gases in several different ways, and some types of farming cause more problems than others.

LAND FOR FARMING

One big problem is that to make space for farms, we have to take over natural, wild land, which often means cutting down forests. Trees store a lot of carbon (see page 10–11). When they are cut down, trees release carbon dioxide as they rot away. Sometimes, farmers burn forests to clear space, and that releases a lot of carbon dioxide too.

Farm crops also store carbon, but not as much as trees, as they're usually much smaller and don't live as long.

ON FIRE

In 2019, huge fires in the Amazon rainforest in South America hit the headlines, as farmers burned down trees to make way for farmland.

NOT ENOUGH SPACE

Hundreds of years ago, there were far fewer people so we had space for all the farms we needed, and still had plenty of wild forests too. But as the world's population zooms up, we need more and more food, and more and more farmland.

The Earth's land area

60% AROUND 12,000 YEARS AGO

Forests

People first began farming around 12,000 years ago. Before that, forests covered more than 60 per cent of the Earth's land. Today, it's fallen to about 30 per cent.

30% TODAY

ANIMAL FARMS

When it comes to climate change, not all farming is the same. Farming animals for meat uses up much more land, energy and water than growing crops as food, and releases more greenhouse gases. Farm animals, especially cows, release a lot of methane, a powerful greenhouse gas, from their bodies (see page 7).

BEEF EMISSIONS

Producing **1 KG** of beef releases an equivalent amount of greenhouse gas to farming...

9 KG OF POTATOES

14 KG OF NUTS

27 KG OF LENTILS

15

CHANGING THE WEATHER

When people think of global warming, they often think of warmer weather – and this really is happening. As the Earth's average temperature increases, many parts of the world are experiencing record-breaking high temperatures, and more severe heatwaves.

On 28 December 2019, Australia's weather was the hottest ever recorded, with an average maximum temperature of 41.9°C.

The high temperatures contributed to serious wildfires breaking out in many areas.

People cool off in Paris, France during a 2019 heatwave.

GETTING HOTTER

A heatwave is several days or weeks when temperatures are much higher than normal. For example, in December 2019, a heatwave in Australia broke the record for the country's hottest December ever. A heatwave across Europe in July 2019 set record temperatures in several different countries. If you live somewhere chilly, a heatwave might sound nice. But heatwaves are actually the most dangerous type of weather. In some heatwaves, thousands of people, especially the elderly and unwell, can die from overheating or dehydration.

WEIRD WEATHER

Global warming can change the climate in other ways too, depending on where you are. This is sometimes called 'global weirding' – because the weather's not always warmer, just weirder, and more extreme. For example...

In deserts and dry places, hotter temperatures heat the land up and dry it out even more, causing droughts.

But some coastal areas get more rain, as extra heat makes more water evaporate from the sea, then fall as rain on the land nearby.

Wind is caused by warm and cool air rising and sinking – so changing temperatures can lead to stronger windstorms.

KNOCK-ON EFFECTS

Extreme weather has other, more long-term effects too. For example, a drought dries out grass and trees, making dangerous wildfires start more easily.

Floods can spread dirty water into clean water supplies, causing disease.

MELTING ICE

Over 70 per cent of the Earth's surface is covered in water. Around the cold North and South Poles, and in high mountain areas, it's often frozen into solid ice sheets and glaciers. But as the world gets warmer, a lot of this ice is melting.

AROUND THE ARCTIC

The Arctic is the area around the North Pole, inside an imaginary line called the Arctic Circle. There's land around the edges, but in the middle is the Arctic Ocean, which is frozen in winter. Each summer, the sea ice partly melts. Since global warming began, it's been melting more and more.

MELTING GLACIERS

Glaciers and ice sheets on land are also melting more than they used to (see pages 20–21). This has been exacerbated by the albedo effect (right). If temperatures keep rising, a lot of the ice in Greenland and the Antarctic could melt, pouring water into the sea.

SEA LEVELS

Melting ice affects the whole planet by making the sea level rise. Since 1880, as the average temperature has risen by almost 1°C, the sea level has risen by about 23 cm. But this will increase, as ice takes time to melt. And, as the sea warms up, it expands, taking up more space. Some scientists think each 1°C could result in a sea level rise of 2–3 m.

As ice melts, it creates a feedback loop, causing even more melting. Here's how it works:

Seawater flooding onto the land in Sandgate, Brisbane, Australia.

THE ALBEDO EFFECT

1 Ice reflects sunlight back out into space, helping to keep the world cooler.

2 As ice melts, the Earth's reflectiveness, or 'albedo' drops.

3 The sea and land soak up more sunlight, and get even warmer – and even more ice melts.

19

CASE STUDY
OKJÖKULL GLACIER

As world ice melts, some ice masses have already disappeared. One example of this is Okjökull, a glacier in Iceland. After shrinking for several years, it was officially declared to be no longer a glacier in 2014.

ICELAND

Site of Okjökull glacier

WHAT IS A GLACIER?

A glacier is a huge, thick mass of slow-moving ice. Glaciers form in cold places where there's a lot of snow, such as the polar regions and high mountains. Layers of snow pack down into solid ice, which then flows very slowly downhill.

Snow falls here.

Snow packs into solid ice.

Ice slowly flows downhill.

At the lower end, the ice melts into streams and rivers.

HOW A GLACIER FORMS

20

SHRINKING OKJÖKULL

Okjökull, meaning 'Ok's glacier', was a small glacier on a volcano named Ok in the west of Iceland. One hundred years ago, it had an area of over 15 square km, but by 2019, it had almost disappeared.

Okjökull in 1986...

...and in 2019, when it had been renamed simply 'Ok'.

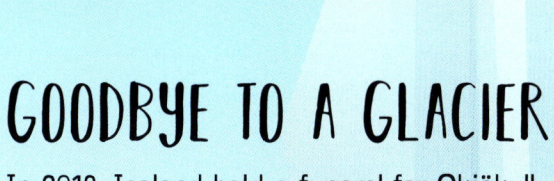

GOODBYE TO A GLACIER

In 2019, Iceland held a funeral for Okjökull. The country's president, along with climate scientists and campaigners, climbed up the Ok volcano to take part in a special ceremony, with speeches about climate change. As well as remembering the glacier, they hoped the funeral would raise awareness of global warming around the world.

A leading Icelandic writer, Andri Snær Magnason, wrote a dedication for the glacier, called 'A letter to the future'. It was inscribed on a copper plaque in both Icelandic and English, and fixed to a rock on the volcano.

ICE FACTS

About 10% of Earth's land is covered in glaciers and ice sheets.

Each year, we are losing around 335 billion tonnes of this ice.

If all the world's glaciers and ice sheets melted, the sea level would rise by 70 m.

IMPACT ON WILDLIFE

Climate change affects weather, land and water around the world. So, not surprisingly, it has a big impact on wild animals and plants too. It affects different species in different ways, depending on where they live, what they eat and many other things. Here are some examples...

POLAR BEAR

Polar bears need Arctic sea ice to travel across and hunt on. As the ice melts and breaks up, it's harder for them to find food.

ANTARCTIC KRILL

Krill are small shrimp-like sea creatures. They shelter under sea ice and feed on algae that grow on it. Their numbers are falling as sea ice melts.

AFRICAN ELEPHANT

Elephants can walk a long way to find drinking water. But as droughts get worse and deserts get bigger, it can be hard for them to find enough.

GREEN TURTLE

Turtles lay their eggs on sandy beaches. Rising sea levels and more powerful storms damage the beaches and reduce the space they have to nest in.

PACIFIC SALMON

Salmon need cold, fast-flowing water to lay their eggs in. Warmer water, or streams drying up, can stop them from breeding.

KOALAS

Rising CO_2 levels are making koalas' food of eucalyptus leaves less nutritious, while increasing droughts and bush fires threaten their habitat.

ECOSYSTEMS

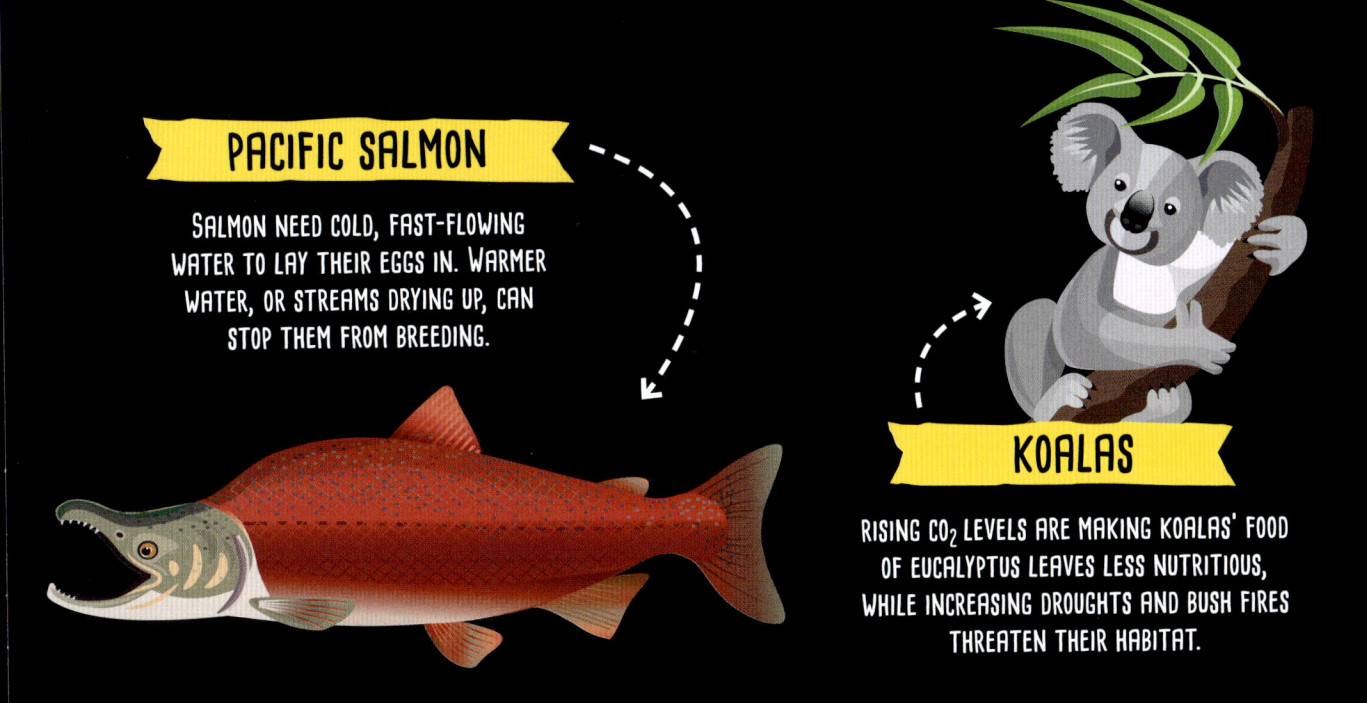

Living things don't just survive on their own — they live in ecosystems. This means each living thing shares its habitat with others, and they depend on each other for food. For example, in the Antarctic, seals and penguins feed on krill, and other animals, such as orcas, feed on them. So when one species, such as krill, falls in number, it affects the others too.

This is a food web in the Southern Ocean, around the Antarctic. It shows a network of species and which feed on which.

PHYTOPLANKTON

ORCA

PENGUIN

KRILL

SEAL

23

CASE STUDY

THE GREAT BARRIER REEF

The Great Barrier Reef is HUGE. It's an enormous strip of thousands of coral reefs and islands, stretching for 2,300 km along the coast of Australia. But it's changing fast, as global warming damages the coral.

Great Barrier Reef

AUSTRALIA

WHAT IS A CORAL REEF?

You can think of a coral reef as a kind of giant seashell. Corals are tiny sea creatures, a bit like very small sea anemones. They live together in big groups, or colonies. As they grow, each colony builds itself a kind of shared shell to live in. Over time, layers of this shell, also called coral, build up into large structures, or coral reefs.

Coral animal or polyp

Coral skeleton, or shell

24

CORAL BLEACHING

Coral bleaching can happen when the water gets warmer. Corals have algae inside them, which help them to survive, and give them their bright colours. When the water is too warm, the corals get rid of the algae and turn pale, making them look white or 'bleached'.

Since 2014, several heatwaves have hit the Great Barrier Reef, and it has suffered a lot of coral bleaching. In 2016, a fifth of its coral was affected. Coral can sometimes recover from bleaching, but if it keeps happening, the coral dies, affecting the whole ecosystem.

A bleached coral reef

AND THAT'S NOT ALL!

Climate change affects coral reefs in other ways, too.

★ Some of the extra carbon dioxide in the air dissolves in the sea, making the water more acidic. This can weaken coral.

★ Bigger, stronger ocean storms can damage coral reefs.

THE GREAT BARRIER REEF HAS...

Almost **3,000** coral reefs

900 islands

Over **1,600** species of fish

Over **600** species of coral

IMPACT ON HUMANS

The world is home to a LOT of humans: about 7.8 billion and counting. Global warming is already having a big impact on us, and it's going to get bigger.

HEALTH

Climate change can be seriously bad for your health in lots of ways:

★ Heatwaves cause illnesses and deaths from overheating

★ Warm, still weather lets polluted air collect, causing breathing problems such as asthma

★ Extreme weather, such as floods and storms, can be dangerous and are often deadly

★ In some places, warmer, wetter weather means more disease germs can survive and spread.

Mosquitos spread deadly diseases. They thrive in warm and wet environments.

HOMES AT RISK

Rising sea levels and more powerful storms are causing problems for people who live on islands and coasts. At the moment, 40 per cent of the world's population live within 100 km of the sea. When homes there are damaged or destroyed, they have to move. Droughts, heatwaves and wildfires can also destroy homes.

People from the low-lying Carteret Islands, off Papua New Guinea, building sea defences.

FOOD SUPPLIES

We all need to eat, and our food mostly comes from farming. But droughts, floods, storms, rising temperatures and rising sea levels can all destroy farmland and crops, leaving lots of people with too little food.

WHAT WILL HAPPEN?

If temperatures keep rising as expected, huge numbers of people will end up migrating to find safer, cooler places to live. We could also face severe food shortages and disease epidemics, unless we find some solutions quickly.

CASE STUDY
SUPER TYPHOON HAIYAN

On 7 November 2013, a massive storm, Super Typhoon Haiyan, hit the Philippines. It was one of the most powerful and destructive tropical storms in history.

WHAT IS A TYPHOON?

A typhoon is a type of tropical cyclone – a huge, whirling windstorm. They are called typhoons in the western Pacific, cyclones in the Indian Ocean and hurricanes in the Atlantic. They can form over tropical oceans when the water is at least 27°C. Vast amounts of water evaporate, forming clouds that swirl around in a wide spiral. If the storm reaches land, it forces huge waves ashore and batters the coast with heavy wind and rain.

A satellite image of Typhoon Haiyan approaching the Philippines.

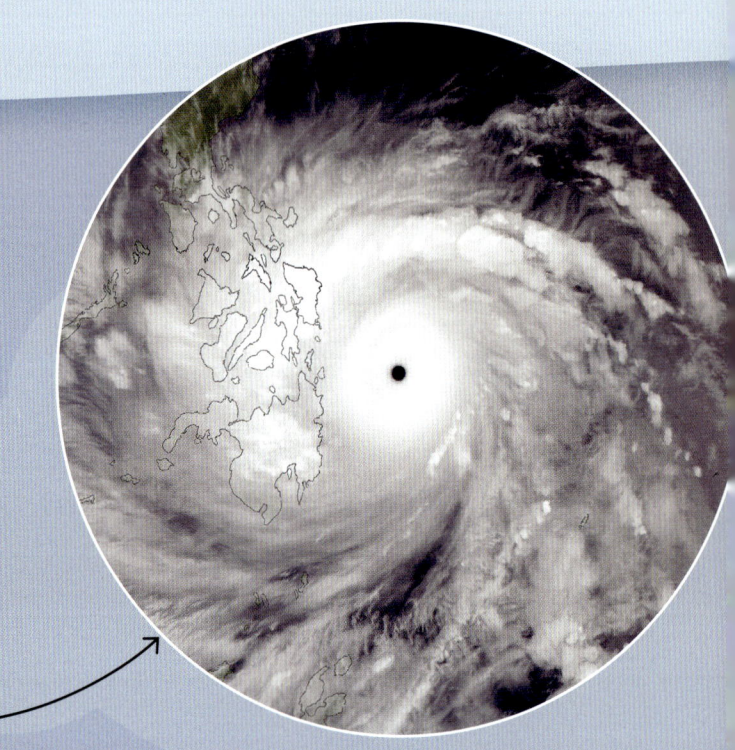

DISASTER STRIKES

As Typhoon Haiyan struck land, it spread death and disaster over a wide area. Winds of over 300 km/h flattened buildings and uprooted trees. Waves up to 7 m high flooded the land with seawater, and the storm clouds dumped almost 30 cm of rain in one day, adding to the floods. The city of Tacloban (right), and many other areas, were largely destroyed.

- Wind speeds: up to 305 km/h
- Death toll: over 6,300
- **TYPHOON HAIYAN**
- People made homeless: 1.9 million
- Cost of rebuilding: over £4 billion

Climate scientists think tropical cyclones will get worse in the future. By the time you read this, an even bigger storm than Haiyan could have broken all the records.

IS CLIMATE CHANGE TO BLAME?

There have always been typhoons and hurricanes, so it's hard to say whether global warming has caused any particular storm, such as Haiyan. But we do know that tropical cyclones begin when the ocean is warm. As sea temperatures rise, these storms seem to be getting stronger, often setting new records for their power, wind speed and destructiveness.

WHAT CAN THE WORLD DO?

Climate change and global warming can seem very scary – and they are. But the world is trying to take action. To fix the problem, all the different countries and their governments have to work together to make plans and stick to them.

TEMPERATURE TARGET

Since 1992, the United Nations has been holding international climate change meetings to agree on ways to fight global warming. In 2015, at a conference in Paris, France, the world's countries signed the Paris Agreement. They agreed to do everything possible to limit the total global average temperature increase to less than 2°C.

GREENHOUSE GAS CHALLENGE

To achieve this, we have to MASSIVELY reduce the amount of greenhouse gases being released into the air. It's not enough to slow them down. They have to actually fall by about 80 per cent to keep warming under control.

So what can countries do? Changes they are making include…

- Passing laws to ban fossil-fuel-burning vehicles. For example, France has announced that all petrol and diesel vehicles will be illegal from 2040, and other countries are making similar laws.

- Making companies that release greenhouse gases pay big taxes or fines.

- Helping to pay for businesses and homes to switch to renewable energy.

- Developing renewable energy sources, such as wind, wave, tidal and solar power (see pages 36–37), to replace fossil-fuel-burning power stations.

Unlike a petrol or diesel car, electric vehicles can be powered by clean, renewable energy.

Costa Rica in Central America has switched to a combination of renewable energy sources.

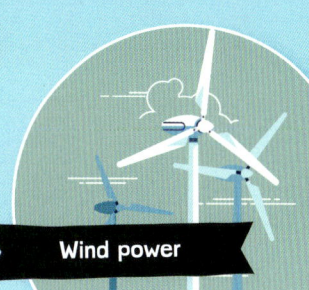

Wind power

Geothermal energy from underground volcanic heat

Hydroelectric power from rivers

Power from the Sun

CAPTURING THE CARBON

It's also important to help remove carbon dioxide from the air, for example by planting trees to help soak up carbon dioxide gas. Countries such as India and Ethiopia have set up enormous tree-planting programs, for example.

On Monday 29 July 2019, over 23 million Ethiopians (more than 20 per cent of the total population) took part in a tree-planting day, and planted over 200 million new trees.

Planting trees can help to remove carbon dioxide from the air.

31

WHAT CAN YOU DO?

It's amazing how many everyday activities add to climate change by releasing greenhouse gases. But that means there are loads of everyday things that you can do to help!

ON THE MOVE

Whenever you can, walk or cycle to get around (as long as you can do so safely). Instead of driving, use buses or trains for longer journeys. Or, if you have to travel by car, arrange to car-share if possible, so that fewer cars are on the road.

GREEN GARDEN

If you have a garden, keep it green! Grass, plants and trees absorb carbon dioxide, so they're much better for the climate than paving the garden over. If you have space, plant a new tree. Or if you don't have a garden, ask if your school can make space for one.

AVOID FLYING

Flying is fun, but very bad for the planet (at least until electric planes take over). Going on a holiday closer to home, by train or ferry, saves lots of emissions.

ONE 3-HOUR FLIGHT PRODUCES AROUND 1 TONNE OF GREENHOUSE GASES PER PERSON – AS MUCH AS LEAVING YOUR COMPUTER SWITCHED ON FOR 10 YEARS!

SAVE ENERGY

Many homes still have gas heating, and electricity often comes from fossil fuels. So you can reduce emissions by using less energy.

★ Switch off lights and electrical appliances when not in use.

★ Hang washing out to dry if possible, instead of tumble-drying.

★ Don't have super-long showers – keep them to 5 minutes.

★ Turn down the heating, and wash clothes at lower temperatures.

GOING SHOPPING

When you're food shopping, choose local fruit and veg that haven't had to travel far. Meat farming releases a lot of carbon, so buying less meat helps too. Avoid 'fast fashion' and look for second-hand and vintage clothes, furniture and kitchen items.

TRANSPORT REVOLUTION

We're used to zooming around the planet in cars, trains and planes that emit greenhouse gases. This has to change. As well as changing *how* we travel, we have to do it less.

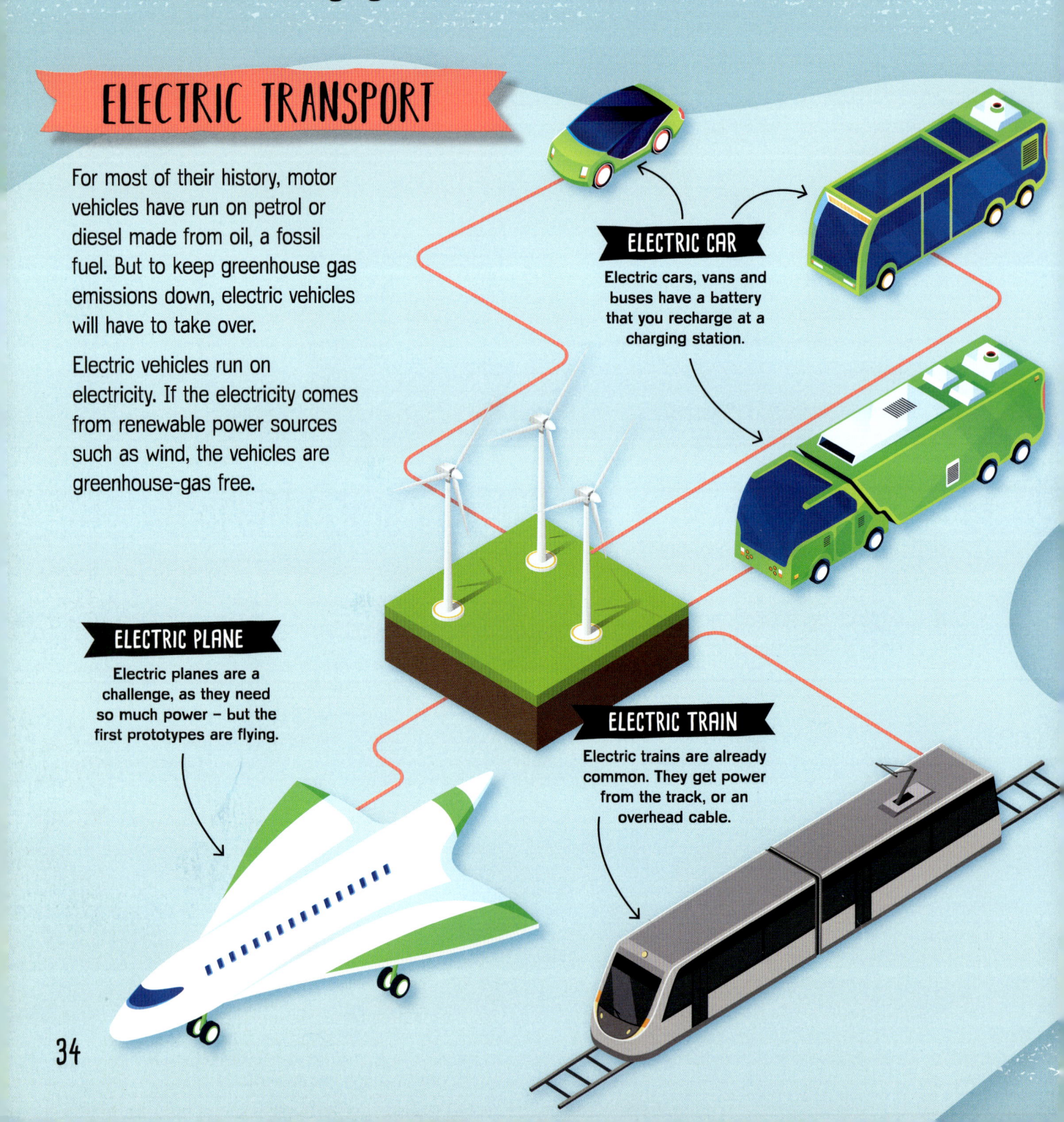

ELECTRIC TRANSPORT

For most of their history, motor vehicles have run on petrol or diesel made from oil, a fossil fuel. But to keep greenhouse gas emissions down, electric vehicles will have to take over.

Electric vehicles run on electricity. If the electricity comes from renewable power sources such as wind, the vehicles are greenhouse-gas free.

ELECTRIC CAR
Electric cars, vans and buses have a battery that you recharge at a charging station.

ELECTRIC PLANE
Electric planes are a challenge, as they need so much power – but the first prototypes are flying.

ELECTRIC TRAIN
Electric trains are already common. They get power from the track, or an overhead cable.

PEOPLE POWER

The greenest forms of transport are walking, or riding a bicycle. Gradually we are changing cities and roads to make them safer for walkers and cyclists. These forms of transport also help you stay healthy, too!

Many cities are building new cycle paths and routes.

1.2 billion ...Number of cars in the world

30 million ...Total length of the world's roads in km

20 per cent ...Percentage of greenhouse gases that come from transport

JUST DON'T GO!

Millions of people travel to and from work and meetings. But a lot of these journeys don't have to happen. Thanks to the internet, more people can work from home and have video conferences instead of real-life meet-ups.

POWER SOURCES

Whenever you plug in a tablet, kettle or printer, you're using electricity to make it work. If that electricity comes from a power station that burns fossil fuels, then it's adding to greenhouse gases and global warming.

RENEWABLES

We need to stop burning fuel to generate electricity, and use renewable and green energy sources instead. These are sources of energy that don't get used up, and don't emit greenhouse gases.

Wind farms use wind to turn turbines, which convert the movement into a flow of electricity.

A hydroelectric power plant uses the downhill flow of a river to turn the turbines.

Solar panels contain materials that collect sunlight and convert it into electricity.

Geothermal plants use heat from deep underground to make electricity.

MORE METHODS

We're developing other types of renewables too. For example, turbines that collect energy from waves and tides are being installed – perfect for countries with a long coastline.

Tidal turbines capture energy from the tide flowing in and out.

The lights at this sports pitch in Rio de Janeiro, Brazil, are powered by solar panels and by special tiles that store the players' movement and convert it into energy.

GREEN WORLD

Climate scientists say that the whole world's energy supplies need to be 100 per cent renewable by the year 2050 at the latest. A few countries, such as Norway and Costa Rica, already get most of their electricity from renewables. But we'll have to change much faster from now on.

FUTURE FARMING

We can travel less, use less energy and buy less stuff. But we can't stop farming, because unlike some things, we really do need food! Instead of stopping, farming has to change.

NO MORE MEAT?

Farming animals, especially cows, produces lots of greenhouse gases but there are no easy answers. We could just grow plants for food. This is unpopular, as many people don't want to give up meat and dairy products. And in some parts of the world the land is good for grazing animals but no good for growing crops.

One solution being explored is growing meat and milk in labs, using a few animal cells.

Lab-grown meat isn't widespread yet, but it could take over from farming large animals.

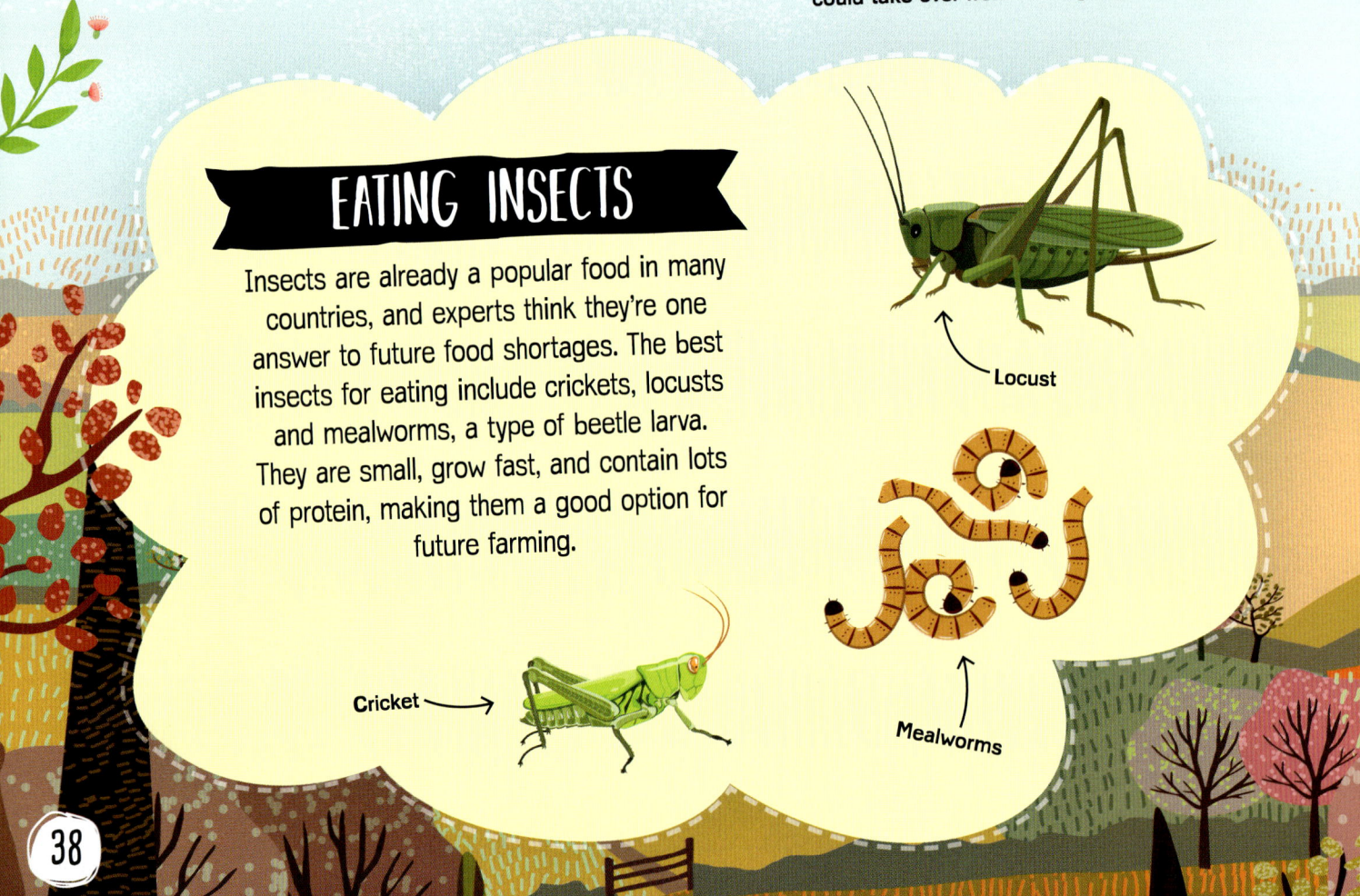

EATING INSECTS

Insects are already a popular food in many countries, and experts think they're one answer to future food shortages. The best insects for eating include crickets, locusts and mealworms, a type of beetle larva. They are small, grow fast, and contain lots of protein, making them a good option for future farming.

Locust

Cricket

Mealworms

VERTICAL FARMS

A vertical farm is an indoor farm, like a tall greenhouse. Crops are grown in layers of trays fed with water and nutrients. As the farm is enclosed, the plants are protected from pests and weather. And as they don't take up much space, we could put vertical farms in cities, so the crops would not have to travel long distances to the shops.

A VERTICAL FARM COULD LOOK LIKE THIS

Water supply

Crops such as salad leaves and tomatoes

CARBON FARMING

On traditional farms, farmers can lock away carbon using 'carbon farming' methods. For example, an egg farmer could plant fruit trees, and let the chickens roam among them. The trees soak up carbon dioxide, and also produce fruit, such as apples and pears.

SCIENCE SOLUTIONS

There might be other solutions to global warming, too. Scientists are developing a range of ideas and inventions that could help the Earth cool back down again, using the latest technology.

ARTIFICIAL TREES

Planting plenty of real trees is important, but artificial trees could also help. They are made of materials that soak up carbon dioxide even faster than a real tree. The gas can then be collected and stored, or used to make other useful things.

Space shade

SPACE SHADE

Another plan is to block out some sunlight with a giant screen in space, to help the Earth cool. It would be very expensive, but there are lots of ideas for making it work. One is to use billions of small flying robots that could assemble the shade in orbit. Or we could use large, thin sheets that would also work as solar panels, providing energy as well as shading the planet.

Carbon dioxide in

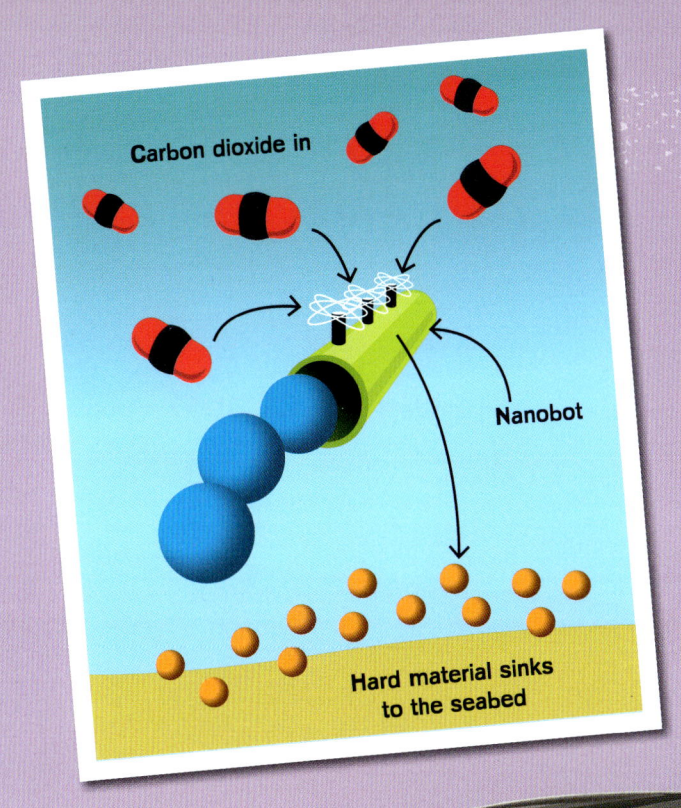

Nanobot

Hard material sinks to the seabed

IN THE SEA

Too much carbon dioxide is a problem in the sea, as well as in the air. One team of scientists has invented a nanobot, or tiny robot, that can suck carbon dioxide out of the water, and use a chemical reaction to turn it into a shell-like material. Millions of the bots could be released into the sea to roam around and reduce the carbon dioxide level.

Future types of fuel may produce no greenhouse gases or pollution.

STORING THE CARBON

If we do manage to remove enough carbon dioxide from the atmosphere, we'll have to put it somewhere. It can be stored underground, or combined with other ingredients to make rock, bricks, strong carbon fibre, or even fuel. These things could be used for:

MAKING ARTIFICIAL TREES, SPACE SHADES OR OTHER INVENTIONS

BUILDING SEA WALLS OR ARTIFICIAL LAND, TO COMBAT RISING SEA LEVELS

MAKING NEW TYPES OF CLEAN FUEL TO BE USED IN PLANES AND ROCKETS

A COOLER FUTURE?

Is it too late? Are we really heading for worldwide disaster as the planet gets hotter and hotter? Or could there still be a happy ending?

WHAT THE SCIENTISTS SAY

The people who really know best are climate scientists. They are busy measuring, tracking and studying global warming and all its effects. And almost all of them agree that the world really is getting warmer, humans really have caused it, and we need to fix it as soon as possible.

Climate scientists carry out research at a frozen lake in Antarctica.

CLIMATE CLASHES

Despite this, there are still some people who don't accept that climate change is a problem. Some say it's just a scare story. Some politicians want to resist changes that could be bad for businesses, or unpopular with voters. And others point out that many developing countries and poorer people can't afford to make big changes. So there are still debates and disagreements about what to do.

Climate change protests, such as those organised by the group Extinction Rebellion, are increasing. They help raise awareness and make sure climate change is covered in the media.

MAKING IT HAPPEN

Individual actions, like flying and driving less, buying less meat and saving energy are a great start. But overall, they aren't enough to fix the problem.

Governments and world organisations need to make the really big changes, and pay for the solutions. So, in countries where people elect their leaders, choosing governments with green policies is helpful too.

DON'T PANIC!

You might find global warming very worrying – and it is reasonable to be alarmed. But there is a lot we can do, and the battle against climate change is already well underway.

With enough co-operation, money and ideas, there's a good chance we can make the changes we need to, and the world can recover. Afterwards, if we can do it, it should be a greener, safer world, too.

GLOSSARY

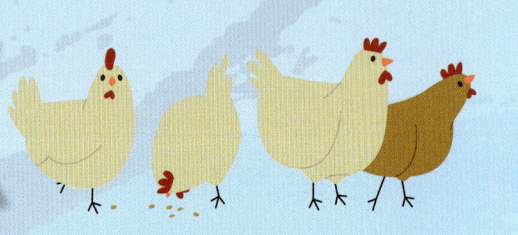

Albedo The whiteness of a surface, and the amount of light that is reflected from it.

Algae Plant-like living things, often with only one cell.

Carbon A natural element found in living things, and also in pencils, diamonds and charcoal.

Carbon dioxide (CO_2) A gas found in the air, and released when carbon-based fuels burn.

Carbon farming Farming in ways that help to reduce the amount of carbon dioxide being released into the air.

Climate The typical or average weather in a particular place, or on Earth as a whole.

Climate change A long-term change in climate patterns.

Coral A hard, shell-like material made by tiny sea creatures, which are also called corals.

Coral bleaching Whitening of coral that happens when corals are stressed and lose the algae that live in their bodies.

Coral polyp The name for an individual coral animal, which is similar to a tiny sea anemone.

Coral reef A large structure in the sea made from a build-up of coral over many years.

Coral skeleton The hard, shell-like part of corals, which is left behind after they die.

Cyclone The name usually given to a tropical cyclone in the Indian Ocean or the southern Pacific.

Diesel A type of fossil fuel made from oil and used in some vehicle engines.

Ecosystem A particular area or place and all the living things that are found there.

Elements The basic substances that matter is made from, such as iron, gold, oxygen and carbon.

Emissions Gases or other substances that are released from something.

Energy The power to make things happen or do work.

Epidemic The spread of a disease through a large number of people.

Food web A diagram showing which living things feed on which others in an ecosystem.

Fossil fuels Fuels such as coal, oil and gas, formed underground from animals or plants that died long ago.

Geothermal energy Heat energy from inside the Earth, which can be used to produce electricity.

Glacier A large slow-moving mass of ice on a mountain or in a polar area.

Global warming A gradual increase in Earth's average temperature over the last two centuries, caused by human activities.

Global weirding Changes in weather patterns related to global warming, including greater extremes of temperature, rainfall and wind.

Greenhouse effect The way some gases in the Earth's atmosphere trap heat, increasing global warming.

Greenhouse gases Gases that contribute to the greenhouse effect, such as carbon dioxide and methane.

Habitat The natural home or surroundings of a living thing.

Heatwave A period of unusually hot weather, usually during the summer.

Hurricane The name usually given to a tropical cyclone in the Atlantic Ocean.

Hydroelectric power Electricity produced from the movement of flowing water.

Ice age A long period in Earth's history when temperatures around the world were unusually cold, resulting in large amounts of ice forming.

Ice sheet A huge sheet of ice covering a large area of land.

Industrial Revolution The period in the 18th and 19th centuries in Europe and the USA when people began to use machines powered by engines to do work and for transport, and the number of factories grew rapidly.

Methane A greenhouse gas often used as a fuel, and also produced by farm animals such as cows.

Nitrous oxide A greenhouse gas that is released when some fuels burn and when plant or animal matter decays.

Nutrients Food chemicals that living things need in order to live and grow.

Oxygen A gas found in the air, which animals breathe in to make their cells work.

Petrol (Also called gasoline) A type of fossil fuel made from oil and used in some vehicle engines.

Phytoplankton Various types of microscopic plant-like living things found in water.

Renewable energy Energy sources that do not run out, such as wind, waves and sunshine.

Solar panel A panel of material that converts sunlight into an electric current.

Species The scientific name for a particular type of living thing.

Tidal turbine A turbine powered by the flow of the tide.

Tropical cyclone A large, spiral-shaped windstorm that forms over warm tropical oceans.

Turbine A device that uses a movement such as the flow of wind or water to make a wheel spin, which is then used to generate electricity.

Typhoon The name usually given to a tropical cyclone in the northern Pacific Ocean.

Vertical farm An indoor farm where crop plants are grown in trays on several levels.

Wildfire A fire burning out of control across a large area, especially in the wilderness or countryside.

Wind turbine A turbine powered by the wind.

FURTHER INFORMATION

BOOKS

**Climate Change and You:
How Climate Change Affects Your Life**
By Emily Raij (Capstone Press, 2019)

A book about the impacts changes in weather and climate have on you, and what you can do to help.

**This Book Will (Help) Cool the Climate:
50 Ways to Cut Pollution, Speak Up and Protect Our Planet!**
By Isabel Thomas (Wren & Rook, 2020)

Lots of easy, fun, practical and thoughtful ways to combat and campaign against climate change and global warming.

Climate Change: The Science Behind Melting Glaciers and Warming Oceans
with Hands-On Science Activities
By Josh Sneiderman (Nomad Press, 2020)

An in-depth exploration of the science behind climate change, including activities and experiments you can do yourself.

**Understanding Global Warming with Max Axiom, Super Scientist 4D:
An Augmented Reading Science Experience**
By Agnieszka Biskup (Capstone Press, 2019)

Graphic-novel-style book all about global warming, with activities, creative ideas and a link to a free 4D augmented reality app.

**Guardians of the Planet:
How to be an Eco-Hero**
By Clive Gifford and Jonathan Woodward (Buster Books, 2019)

How to help the planet with a wide variety of activities, projects and everyday habits, from helping wildlife and cleaning up the coast to running a green home.

WEBSITES

https://climatekids.nasa.gov/climate-change-meaning
NASA's Climate Kids website, with lots of facts, videos, activities and games.

https://www.energystar.gov/ia/products/globalwarming/downloads/ GoGreen_Activities%20508_compliant_small.pdf
Printout with a family carbon calculator, useful tips and Go Green Action cards to make and play.

https://www.amnh.org/explore/ology/climate-change#all
American Museum of Natural History's Climate Change site, with information, pictures, puzzles and quizzes.

WATCH

Climate Change – The Facts
(2019) by Serena Davies, presented by Sir David Attenborough
A round-up of climate change science, solutions and dangers with leading TV naturalist Sir David Attenborough. Watch it online at:
https://www.bbc.co.uk/programmes/m00049b1

Anthropocene: The Human Epoch
(2018) (12A) by Jennifer Baichwal, Nicholas de Pencier and Edward Burtynsky, narrated by Alicia Vikander
Documentary about the impact of our species on Planet Earth. Available online from Apple, Amazon, Kanopy and Google Play.

Before The Flood
(2016) (PG) by Fisher Stevens, presented by Leonardo DiCaprio
In this National Geographic film, actor Leonardo DiCaprio explores climate change impacts around the world.
Find out how to watch the film at:
https://www.beforetheflood.com/screenings

Note to parents and teachers: every effort has been made by the Publishers to ensure websites are suitable for children, that they are of the highest educational value, and that they contain no inappropriate or offensive material. However, because of the nature of the Internet, it is impossible to guarantee that the contents of these sites will not be altered. We strongly advise that Internet access is supervised by a responsible adult.

INDEX

aeroplanes 10, 12–13, 33–34, 41
Amazon rainforest 14
Antarctic 18, 22–23, 42
Arctic 18, 22
atmosphere, Earth's 6, 10–11, 13, 41
Australia 16, 19, 23–25

balloons, hot air 12

carbon storage 11, 14, 31–32, 39–41
cars 4, 9–10, 13, 30–32, 34–35
climate change 4–5, 13, 15, 17, 21–22, 25–26, 29–30, 32, 42–43
coral 24–25
cows 7, 15, 38

diseases 17, 26–27
droughts 5, 17, 22–23, 27

ecosystems 23, 25
effect, albedo 18–19
effect, greenhouse 6–7
 and throughout
electricity 9–10, 31, 33–34, 36–37
energy
 new forms of energy 30, 41
 renewable 30–31, 33–34, 36–37
 using less energy 33, 43
epidemics 27
Ethiopia 31
Extinction Rebellion 42

factories 4, 7–10
farming 7, 9, 14–15, 27, 38–39
 carbon farming 39
 clearing forests 14–15
 farming insects 38
 future farming 38–39
 land use 14–15, 39
 livestock farming 7, 15, 33, 38
 vertical farms 39

floods 5, 17, 19, 26–28
flying 12–13, 33–34, 43
forests 14–15
fuels, fossil 4, 7, 9–13, 30–31, 33–34, 36

gases, greenhouse 4, 6–15, 30–36, 38, 40–41
 carbon dioxide 7, 10–11, 14, 25, 31–33, 39–41
 methane 7, 15
 nitrous oxide 7
glaciers 18
 Okjökull glacier 20–21
global warming 4–9
 causes of 4–15
 effects of 4–5, 16–29
 solutions and actions 30–43
Great Barrier Reef 24–25
 coral bleaching 25
Greenland 18

heatwaves 16, 25–27
hurricanes 28–29

ice, melting 5, 18–22
Iceland 20–21
Industrial Revolution 8–9

land use 9, 14–15

Magnason, Andri Snær 21

Philippines 28–29
planes see aeroplanes
population, human 8–9, 15, 26–27
power stations 4, 10, 30, 36

reefs, coral 24–25

scientists, climate 29–30, 37, 42
seas
 carbon dioxide in sea 11, 25, 41
 sea level rises 5, 18–22, 27, 40–41

space shades 40–41
storms 5, 17, 22–23, 25–29

temperature, Earth's 4–6, 16–19, 27, 30, 40, 42
trains 9, 13, 32–34
trees 10, 14, 17, 28, 30–33, 39–41
 artificial 40–41
 planting programs 31, 40
Typhoon Haiyan 28–29

United Nations 30
 Paris Agreement 30

weather
 changing 4–5, 16–17, 22–23, 26–29
 global weirding 17
wildfires 5, 16–17, 23, 27
wildlife 22–25
Wright Flyer 12

48

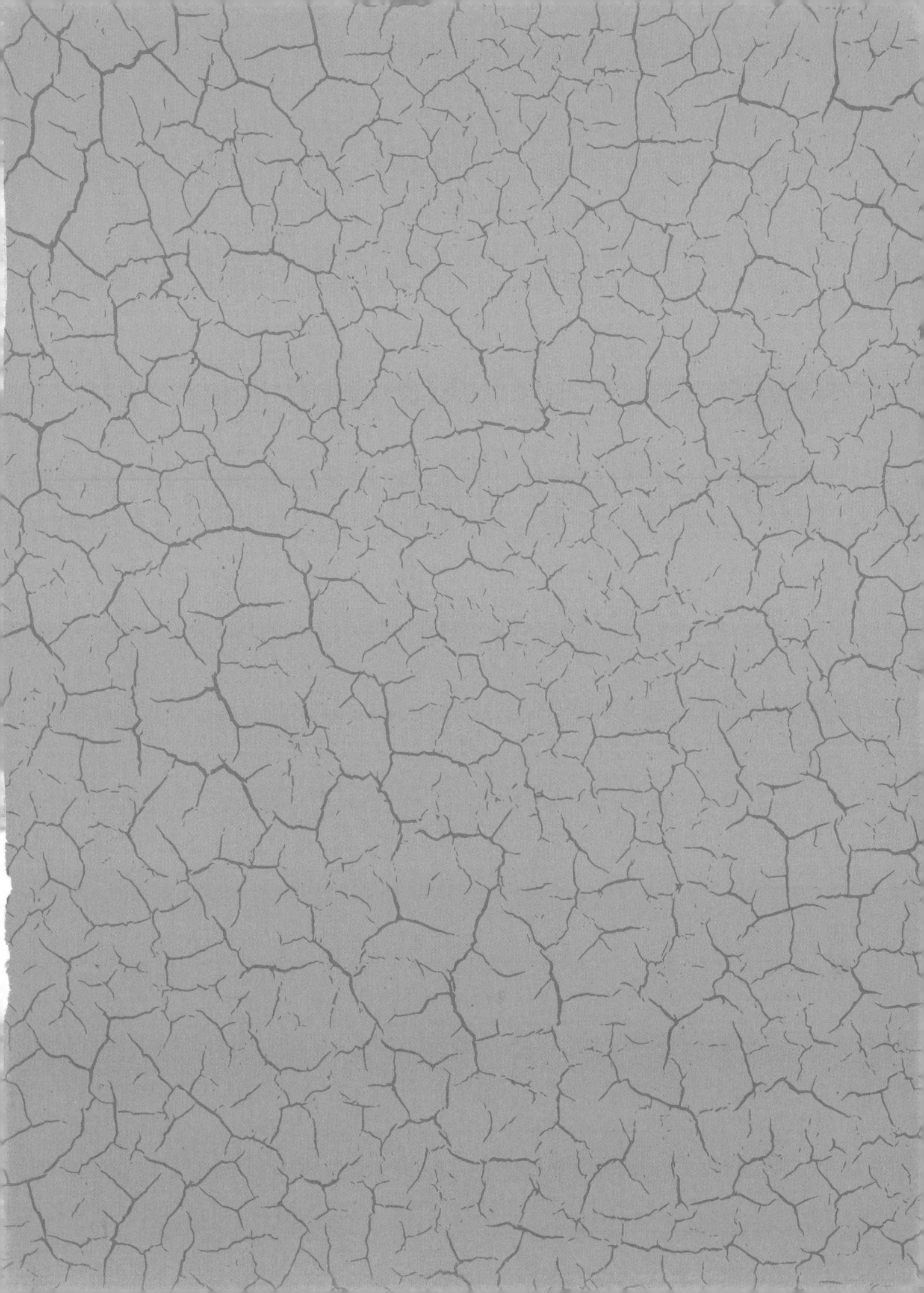

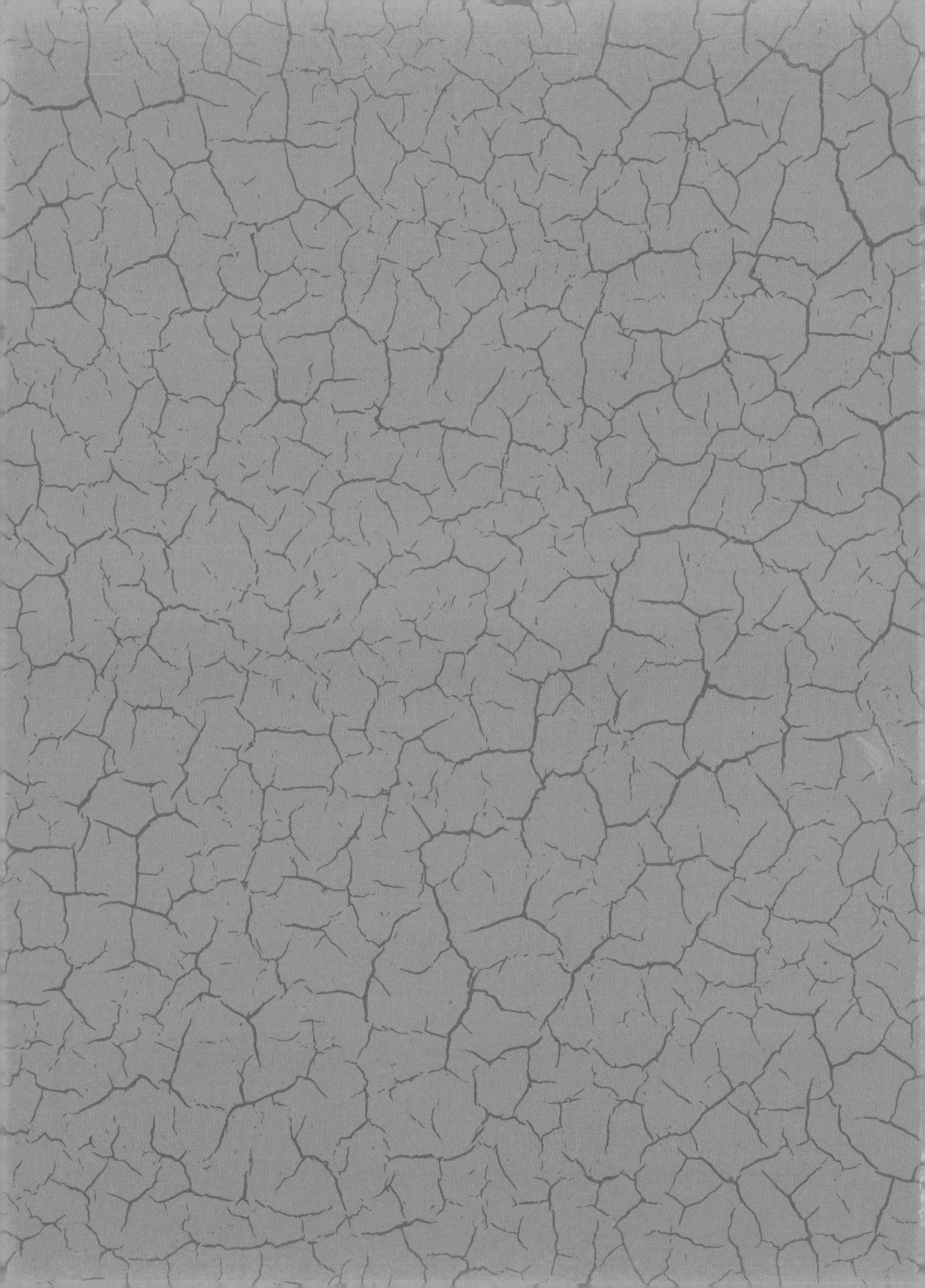